THE
GRAMMAR
OF GOD

בְּנִים לַיּוֹם הַשְּׁלִשִׁי כִּי וּבַיּוֹם הַשְּׁלִשִׁי יֵרֵד יְהוָה

לְעֵינֵי כָל־הָעָם עַל־הַר סִינָי׃ וְהִגְבַּלְתָּ אֶת־הָעָם סָבִיב ל

הִשָּׁמְרוּ לָכֶם עֲלוֹת בָּהָר וּנְגֹעַ בְּקָצֵהוּ כָּל־הַנֹּגֵעַ

בָהָר מוֹת יוּמָת׃ לֹא־תִגַּע בּוֹ יָד כִּי־סָקוֹל יִסָּקֵל אוֹ־יָרֹה

אִם־בְּהֵמָה אִם־אִישׁ לֹא יִחְיֶה בִּמְשֹׁךְ הַיֹּבֵל הֵמָּה

יַעֲלוּ בָהָר׃ וַיֵּרֶד מֹשֶׁה מִן־הָהָר אֶל־הָעָם וַיְקַדֵּשׁ אֶת

הָעָם וַיְכַבְּסוּ שִׂמְלֹתָם׃ וַיֹּאמֶר אֶל־הָעָם הֱיוּ נְכֹנִים לִשְׁלֹ

שֶׁת יָמִים אַל־תִּגְּשׁוּ אֶל־אִשָּׁה׃ וַיְהִי בַיּוֹם הַשְּׁלִישִׁי בִּ

הְיֹת הַבֹּקֶר וַיְהִי קֹלֹת וּבְרָקִים וְעָנָן כָּבֵד עַל־הָהָר וְקֹל

שֹׁפָר חָזָק מְאֹד וַיֶּחֱרַד כָּל־הָעָם אֲשֶׁר בַּמַּחֲנֶה׃ וַיּוֹצֵא מֹ

שֶׁה אֶת־הָעָם לִקְרַאת הָאֱלֹהִים מִן־הַמַּחֲנֶה וַיִּתְיַצְּבוּ בְּתַחְתִּית

הָהָר׃ וְהַר סִינַי עָשַׁן כֻּלּוֹ מִפְּנֵי אֲשֶׁר יָרַד עָלָיו יְ

הוָה בָּאֵשׁ וַיַּעַל עֲשָׁנוֹ כְּעֶשֶׁן הַכִּבְשָׁן וַיֶּחֱרַד כָּל־הָהָר מְ

אֹד׃ וַיְהִי קוֹל הַשֹּׁפָר הוֹלֵךְ וְחָזֵק מְאֹד מֹשֶׁה יְדַבֵּר וְהָאֱ

לֹהִים יַעֲנֶנּוּ בְקוֹל׃ וַיֵּרֶד יְהוָה עַל־הַר סִינַי אֶל־רֹאשׁ

הָהָר וַיִּקְרָא יְהוָה לְמֹשֶׁה אֶל־רֹאשׁ הָהָר וַיַּעַל מֹשֶׁה׃ וַ

יֹּאמֶר יְהוָה אֶל־מֹשֶׁה רֵד הָעֵד בָּעָם פֶּן־יֶהֶרְסוּ אֶל־יְהוָה לִ

רְאוֹת וְנָפַל מִמֶּנּוּ רָב׃ וְגַם הַכֹּהֲנִים הַנִּגָּשִׁים אֶל־יְהוָה יִתְקַ

דָּשׁוּ פֶּן־יִפְרֹץ בָּהֶם יְהוָה׃ וַיֹּאמֶר מֹשֶׁה אֶל־יְהוָה לֹא־יוּ

כַל הָעָם לַעֲלֹת אֶל־הַר סִינָי כִּי־אַתָּה הַעֵדֹתָה בָּנוּ לֵא

מֹר הַגְבֵּל אֶת־הָהָר וְקִדַּשְׁתּוֹ׃ וַיֹּאמֶר אֵלָיו יְהוָה לֶךְ

רֵד וְעָלִיתָ אַתָּה וְאַהֲרֹן עִמָּךְ וְהַכֹּהֲנִים וְהָעָם אַל

THE GRAMMAR OF GOD

*A Journey into the Words
and Worlds of the Bible*

———◆———

AVIYA KUSHNER

SPIEGEL & GRAU / NEW YORK

Published in the United States by Spiegel & Grau, an imprint of Random House,
a division of Penguin Random House LLC, New York.

SPIEGEL & GRAU and the HOUSE colophon are registered trademarks of
Penguin Random House LLC.

An earlier version of the chapter entitled "Laughter" was previously published under the
title "I'm Not Crazy About That Part" in *A Public Space*.

Library of Congress Cataloging-in-Publication Data

Kushner, Aviya.
The grammar of God : a journey into the words and worlds of the Bible / Aviya Kushner.
pages   cm
Includes bibliographical references and index.
ISBN 978-0-385-52082-9
eBook ISBN 978-0-679-64526-9
1. Bible—Criticism, Textual.   2. Bible—Translating.   3. Kushner, Aviya—
Religious life.   I. Title.
BS471.K87 2015
220.4—dc23   2014033822

Printed in the United States of America on acid-free paper

randomhousebooks.com

spiegelandgrau.com

2 4 6 8 9 7 5 3 1

First Edition

Book design by Susan Turner

לאמא ואבא
For my mother and father

Grammar is a form of history.

DEREK WALCOTT,
What the Twilight Says

CONTENTS

How It All Began

In the hot August of 2002, when the world was still wob-
bling from the shock of the September 11 attacks, I drove to
Iowa with a name in my pocket. I was about to start graduate
school, and that scribbled name was the only guidance I had in the
thousand-mile journey from New York. It reassured me as I drove
past cities, flat fields, and the Mississippi River, then through
miles and miles of tall corn. After years of devoting myself to poetry, I was about to start a graduate program in nonfiction writing.
On the first day of classes, I went to find the teacher whose name I
had been carrying, but I mistakenly arrived at the end of her class
instead of at the beginning.

As I listened to the last five minutes of class from the hallway,
I thought of a story I had been taught as a child. An old man was
too poor to pay for school, so he climbed onto the roof of a yeshiva to learn the Torah. The man became the great sage Hillel,
but as a student, he had no choice but to eavesdrop. For the first
time I fully understood that Talmudic story. I realized it made no
difference whether I was in the room or out of it. I understood
that it did not matter whether I had come to Iowa to study non-

fiction or poetry, or that two poets had sent me to this particular teacher. It did not matter how old I was, or how tired I felt. All that mattered was that I continued to learn, in whatever way possible: in the hallway or on the rooftop, if that was what it took.

I did not feel like a traditional graduate student. Though I was only twenty-eight, I already felt a little old, a little weathered. I felt like an interloper in the safe plains of academia. I had just spent two years in Jerusalem, officially as a travel columnist and a financial journalist, but increasingly, as the second intifada raged on, I was asked to interview victims of the crossfire of history and belief and politics. I interviewed the brother of two teenage girls killed by a bomb in a dance club; I walked into poor neighborhoods and spoke with grieving grandmothers. As I traveled dutifully throughout a country in which tourists were then practically extinct, I narrowly escaped being bombed several times; on a few occasions, gunfire came far too close for comfort. Now and then, I traveled to Europe, exploring history's prior battlegrounds in Berlin, or walking Jews' Street in London, writing stories the entire time. I thought I was done with being a student.

But by that hot August, after a year in which the entire world felt overturned, when the tallest buildings of New York crumbled and fell and became ash, I felt a deep desire for safety. And I wanted a second chance to read in the luxurious way a student can. I wanted time. Studying at the University of Iowa, a mecca for young writers with the oldest graduate writing program in the country, was a dream. That teacher I first heard in the hallway, listening and not seeing, was Marilynne Robinson. She usually taught the nineteenth-century writers who meant a great deal to her—Whitman, Dickinson, Emerson, Thoreau, Melville—and I enrolled in those courses. I did not expect that a year later, she would offer a class in the Bible, and that I would take it, too. This meant reading the Bible in English—something I had never done; I had grown up in a Jewish community, reading it in Hebrew. In fact, reading the Christian Bible was widely considered taboo in the small religious town where I grew up.

The first semester focused on the Old Testament, the second on the New Testament. Though Marilynne, as all her students called her, was incredibly learned, I realized she did not have access to certain elements of the Bible—a book she had spent decades with—because she did not read the Bible in Hebrew. Only one of my classmates read Hebrew.

At first, when I seemed surprised or even shocked by what we read or discussed in class, my facial expressions would betray me, and Marilynne would ask: "Why are you so surprised?"

I would say, "I would have to explain so much to you about Hebrew for you to understand why this translation is surprising."

"Try."

I did. I took notes on what surprised me; and those notes became letters that eventually became essays. Eventually, those essays became my master's thesis. I figured that would be the end of it. But one day, when I went to discuss the progress of my thesis, Marilynne closed the door to her office.

There were a few tense seconds while she walked from the door to her chair. Then she sat down and said: "This will be a book."

There was a glass bowl on the table, full of chocolates. We each unwrapped a chocolate and ate it; by the end of our meeting, there would be no more chocolates in the bowl.

I talked about all the reasons why I did not think I could make this personal and rather messy project into a book. I was not a Bible scholar. I did not fit the profile of a Bible obsessive: I was not driven by religious fervor or a desire to convert others, but simply by the love of a book and a language, and a deep wish to give something back to a teacher who had given me so much. But she smiled calmly as if she knew all that lay ahead.

Books choose their writers, I now believe, and not the other way around; I suspect my teacher already knew that. And she asked me to keep one thing in mind: even if the translation was inaccurate at times, and contained errors, she wanted me to remember that the Bible in English is holy to millions and millions of people.

I kept my teacher's directive in mind for years. I knew how much she loved the Bible, how much the English version of it meant to her. I knew that for her it *was* the Bible, not a translation. And gradually I realized that I could not read the translations without remembering the great Hillel on the roof of the yeshiva, as an older man, and all the other stories and cultural breadcrumbs of my life. I could not explain what Hebrew was without writing who I was and where I came from. The translation is holy to millions, but so is the Hebrew I was born into.

I spent time thinking about other readers who had devoted years to the Bible and its mysteries; sadly, many suffered because of their great passion for the text. I often thought of Rabbi Akiva, who began as an illiterate shepherd in the first century and became a major scholar. I kept in mind two aspects of Rabbi Akiva's life. First, that according to Genesis Rabbah 24:7—an important third-century commentary on Genesis attributed to the sage Osha'ya—in a discussion with two other rabbis, Rabbi Akiva insisted that a major principle of the Torah was the commandment from Leviticus 19:18, to love fellow humans.

His attachment to this verse, I imagine, was the product of his humble beginnings; he had learned to see all people as his equals, learned never to look down on another because that person did not know something. After all, he himself was proof that everything could be learned. This attitude of love—and equal access—strikes me as necessary for a teacher, but also, perhaps, for a writer who is trying to convey something important and complicated to another person. It is far easier, I already knew from my work as a journalist, to criticize than to explain, to bash than to build. I knew I had to approach this book with openness and compassion and humility, and not with disdain. As I encountered aspects of Christian thought that I knew nothing about, I had to ask about what I did not understand and not be embarrassed. I had to proceed with love.

But love is not enough. The love of fellow man is only part of Rabbi Akiva's story; it is the story of his life, not his death. And the horribly haunting way Rabbi Akiva died—according to a well-known legend—also stuck with me as I worked: we are told that the Romans flayed his skin with an iron comb. Jewish tradition attributes Rabbi Akiva's brutal murder to his refusal to stop teaching the Torah.

To my chagrin, I soon learned that this frightening and depressing combination of great knowledge and ugly death appears not only in the lives of the rabbis but also in the lives of Christian translators. William Tyndale, whose translation is the foundation of the King James Bible, was strangled and his body burned at the stake. The remains of John Wycliffe, who also worked on an early translation of the Bible into English, were exhumed and thrown into a river. Translation, like scholarship, has long been a life-threatening enterprise. Making something understandable to the general public has meant risking everything, even, as in the case of the great Rabbi Akiva, one's skin.

* * *

THE JOURNEY OF THE BIBLE, both its scholarship and its translations, is full of sacrifices and hardships, torture and death, even disgrace after death. And the Bible's history is also one of stories of teachers and students, of readers who felt that their work—however flawed and however small—was a gift to their fellow humans. It is impossible to have a strong Jewish education and not be aware of the physical sacrifices teachers and students made throughout the centuries to keep the Torah alive; it is equally impossible to read even a little bit of the story of the translation of the Bible into English without understanding that that enterprise, too, was often interwoven with great danger. And, of course, the Bible and its translations—accurate and inaccurate—have been used, throughout history, to incite hatred. It is therefore rare, historically, to be able to read a translation of the Bible simply to know what it says, and to do so in complete freedom.

This is why I so appreciated Marilynne Robinson's willingness to walk me into the Christian Bible, both in the graduate school seminar and in the small community class she offered, her welcoming me into the social room of her own church, with no mission other than to teach. I knew that most people who had grown up as I did, deep in the Jewish community, would never find themselves in either location. This is why the frank conversations between Marilynne and me about moments in the Bible were precious; we were both talking about what we most loved, as openly as we possibly could. We were each taking the other home.

Introduction

◆

WHEN I WAS A CHILD I ASSUMED THAT ALL FAMILIES DISCUSSED the grammar of the Bible in Hebrew at the dining room table. When I entered kindergarten, I heard, to my shock, that most American-born children spoke English; I spoke only Hebrew then. On my first sleepover, I learned that many families did not discuss ancient grammar. Not over dinner, not at all. This struck me as a terrible shame, a missed opportunity, and it still does. In the house I grew up in, the Bible was and is a topic of constant conversation: both the big questions and issues, like how the world began, and the more particular—the roots of what is male and what is female, the names of God, and how various verbs, prepositions, and phrases function. We discussed the Bible's humor, its laws, its wild leaps of narrative, and its rather charming tendency to contradict itself. The conversation often turned to the question that obsessed the tenth-century and eleventh-century Hebrew grammarians of Spain and Babylon (modern-day Iraq): how to define a word that appears only once in the Bible—a question still as slippery and fascinating as ever.

As I moved from my small religious town twenty-five miles from New York City and into the larger world, I realized that most Americans saw the Bible—the text that had animated and informed and enlarged my life—in a way I did not recognize. For years, I thought the disparity between how I read the Bible and how the wider world read it was a private concern, the worry of a child of an Israeli mother and an American father. Eventually, I understood that this particular space between languages matters, that it is more than a personal interest, because the Bible occupies such a large place in both American and world culture, and because it is a source of moral guidance for so many. As I began talking about the difference between the way I read the Bible and the way most Americans encountered it, I learned, to my surprise, that how to read a word or how to understand a quirk of ancient grammar was something other people—religious and secular alike—actually wanted to hear about.

Some of the most politically charged issues of our time are rooted in biblical translation. The commandment "Thou shalt not kill," for instance, is not nearly as straightforward in Hebrew as it is in English. In biblical Hebrew, there is a gaping difference between the verb "to kill"—*laharog*—and the verb "to murder"—*lirtzoach*; the Hebrew word used in the Ten Commandments is "murder," yet the commandment is frequently mistranslated as "Thou shalt not kill." This word choice matters because there are acceptable forms of killing in the Bible (such as self-defense). As I read and reread familiar passages in translation, wondering what effect one word choice might have over another, I realized that defining "murder" is both an ancient and a contemporary question. Many of us are still talking about what constitutes a just war; when, if ever, the death penalty is acceptable; and when, exactly, life begins. When life starts and what murder means are moral questions but also questions of language, because they involve defining the exact boundaries of individual words. When the Bible was translated, these questions of language became questions of translation.

THE PATH I TOOK TO reading the Bible in translation occurred over many years and in many places, from the house I grew up in to Iowa City, but it probably started with Isaiah. As a young poet who had just finished a graduate program in poetry, I was trying to read the best poets I could find. Isaiah, whom I'd read since childhood and had heard sung aloud since infancy, easily held up next to Yeats and Auden and Dylan Thomas. In fact, Isaiah, with his classic mixture of conversation and command, seemed to be the best poet I'd encountered—ever. So I began writing "Isaiah poems" early on Sunday mornings, riffs on individual lines in Isaiah.

The "Isaiah project" quickly seeped into the other days of the week and became something of an obsession. Over the course of six years and moves from Boston to Jerusalem to New York to Iowa City, I wrote Isaiah poems. As bombs fell in Jerusalem I would often reread Isaiah and his descriptions of destruction followed by comfort. The ancient prophet felt contemporary to me, as if he were at my elbow. After leaving Jerusalem to return to the States—on September 11, 2001, of all days, a harrowing experience that included an unexpected grounding in London for ten days and a bomb threat on the plane to New York—I felt even more connected with Isaiah.

It was this fascination with Isaiah that led me to take the graduate course in the Bible with Marilynne Robinson. By then, I was curious, deeply and completely. I wanted to know what the rest of the world heard when they read about God and man, heaven and earth.

I had read the Bible countless times in Hebrew, could easily quote long passages from memory, and a few years prior had read it aloud from beginning to end as a memorial to my grandfather. Reading it in English left me in a new country entirely. I was lost much of the time, and many times saddened at what had been misrepresented or obscured in moving the words from the Hebrew to the English, from the ancient to the more contemporary.

Initially, I was interested only in Isaiah, but quickly enough I had a new obsession: the "Isaiah project" morphed into the "translation project." I soon realized that I needed to read everything: the exciting parts and the so-called boring parts of the Bible. I'd have to read the entire Tanakh—an acronym for Torah, Neviim (Prophets), and Ketuvim (Writings), or what Christians call the Old Testament—in English to get a sense of how the moving between languages might affect meaning. And I would have to commit to the project fully.

And so, one scorching hot Sunday in Iowa City, a small college town sixty-eight miles from the Mississippi River, I moved a shelf of Hebrew Bibles from my house to the trunk of my car. Out went Isaiah, the Psalms, and several editions of the Five Books of Moses. I was trying to see the Bible translated into English for what it was on its own terms, and I wanted to read without Hebrew fighting with English in my ears.

Above all, I had to remove the temptation to dip back into the words I knew and loved. I had to restrain myself from returning to the first words I had ever known, the gorgeous and familiar ancient Hebrew.

In many ways, this book is a chronicle of the largest of the surprises I encountered while reading the Bible in English. During that entire first long read in the quiet of Iowa, with only the Oxford Annotated Bible and the King James Version, I was often in shock, mouth literally open. The relative slowness of Genesis in English amazed me; the change of pace changed meaning, from the creation of the world onward. The changes in tone, too, were frequently astounding. Sometimes the choices were beautiful, sometimes slightly inaccurate, and sometimes just plain wrong.

But perhaps the biggest surprise was the lone voice of the Bible I encountered in English. While it is possible to read the Hebrew Bible with just the text—what is called the *pshat*, literally "the simple or the plain"—that is not how I usually read it, and that is not how it is generally taught in yeshiva classrooms. In school, as a child, I read the Torah from books called *mikraot gedolot*—"great scriptures," also called the Rabbinic Bible in English—volumes in which each page is crammed with commentary surrounding the text of the Bible in different languages, scripts, and fonts. To the side sat the words of Onkelos, a Roman convert to Judaism, whose great first-century translation into Aramaic can be read as a commentary. Beneath the text of the Bible lay Rashi's commentary, expressing his thoughts in his special medieval script. Rashi lived in the eleventh century in what would become France, and his answers never include the question to which he is responding. As a child, I was tested on these absent questions; my task was to imagine what the medieval rabbi had wanted to know.

Around Rashi lay other commentators, rabbis chiming in from their perches in Spain, France, Germany, the Arab world, and Israel, spanning at least twelve centuries. Everything was up for discussion, and from my earliest memory I was taught to demand a second opinion, and a third, and a fourth, to cross borders of time and language in order to hear those multiple voices. The Hebrew text I grew up with is beautifully unruly, often ambiguous, multiple in meaning, and hard to pin down; many of the English translations are, above all, certain.

The difference is especially apparent when it comes to narrative arc, or the basic elements of how we tell stories. Contemporary readers crave a familiar shape to our stories, with a clear ending: introduction of problem, heightening of problem, resolution of problem. That format was created by the ancient Greek dramatists. But the Bible is different: whether a Hebrew or English reader, you'll rarely find tidy stories with logical A to Z progressions in the Bible. The rabbis, who developed certain *klallim*, or "rules of reading," explain this through what they call *ein mukdam u'meuchar baTorah*, a notion that flouts our contemporary sense of order and time: that, literally, there is no early and no late in the Torah. This concept, which first appears in the Mekhilta, or commentary on Exodus, of Rabbi Yishmael (90–135 C.E.), is later mentioned by most of the traditional Jewish commentators. According to this *klal*, the events in the Hebrew Bible are not always written in the order in which they occur; just because an event is written about after another one does not mean it chronologically follows it.

When I was a child, there being no early and no late struck me as bizarre, a way to avoid the chronological difficulties that run rampant in the text of the Bible. I thought it was an easy way out. But now I realize that this "rule" is a key difference between how Jewish thinkers and Christian thinkers understand the Bible, and how they translate it. There is an arc to a Christian reading, and to many English translations, and a search for foreshadowing and "parallels" that are not always there in the original Hebrew. In contrast, in Jewish tradition, the rabbis often insist that the order of events might have been presented in a different way if the Torah had a traditional view of time or narrative. The first and perhaps best-known example occurs in the two differing creation stories presented in Genesis. But the rabbis go beyond addressing just the double-creation issue; they are concerned with whether the Torah should have started with Genesis at all. In his commentary on Genesis 1:1, for instance, Rashi quotes Rabbi Yitzchak, who happens, some say, to also be his own father. Rabbi Yitzchak feels the Torah should have opened not with Genesis but with Exodus 12:2. Why? Because Exodus 12:2 is the first moment when a *mitzvah*, or commandment, is given to the People of Israel. For Rabbi Yitzchak, the story of the Bible truly begins with nationhood—not with the creation of the world. This is part of the centuries-old discussion of what kind of a book the Bible is: a book about the history of the world, a book of law, or the story of a particular nation. Rabbi Yitzchak's insistence that the story begins with nationhood, not creation, is just one of a long series of arguments that snake throughout biblical commentary on how to read events and interpret time.

It may seem heretical to a reader unfamiliar with Torah commentary to encounter all these objections to a book rabbis ostensibly believe was dictated by God and written down by Moses. But the rabbis' fiery comments on narrative order and meaning are not primarily about right and wrong. Instead, their discussion is an attempt to comprehend *how* and *why* the Torah does what it does. Commentary is above all a quest for understanding, and the reader is asked to be imaginative. With an ancient text that repeats and sometimes seems to contradict itself, a willingness to consider various possibilities is essential.

The Hebrew Bible is full of echoes that seem to emphasize the idea that time and event are multifaceted; the creation story, for instance, resonates again in the Book of Isaiah, with images and phrases repeating in a new location. But although Christians read Isaiah as a foreshadowing of Jesus, whose name appears nowhere in the Book of Isaiah, the language of Isaiah actually echoes the language of Genesis. For Jews, the experience of reading is probably more of a going back, not a going forward, and sometimes it is a going around.

Perhaps that centuries-old rule of reading, the idea that there is no early and no late in the Torah, is part of what makes so many readers—and writers—feel attached to the ancient text: this reliance on the reader's judgment and ability to understand and infer includes the reader in the book. How the reader reads matters, no matter what century she lives in, and so she gets to have a say in what the Bible is to her. In the same way that modern art often includes the viewer, the Bible in Hebrew, read closely and with attention, can include the reader to an astonishing extent. I often found myself participating—loudly—in the questions and debates of the rabbis and commentators from various centuries on topics such as order, chronology, narrative pattern, and of course the meaning of a phrase, a section, or a law.

Translation often collapses all of this conversation—the conversation of my entire life—into a one-word summary. Translation means that a translator has picked one word above all the others: one winner, with all the finalists gone from the page forever. Translation always calls upon the translator to make a judgment call, and what the reader hears, then, is a judgment.

THE TEXT FOR THE CLASS at Iowa was the Oxford Annotated Bible, but as my fascination grew, I acquired many other translations. I added the famous King James translation early on, using the 1611 version that is so familiar to English readers. Many scholars have discredited the accuracy of the King James translation, but I was not interested in evaluating the scholarly success of the poetic King James Bible, a text that both stunned and moved me.

I simply wanted to see what my writer friends and teachers were reading, to understand what they meant by "the Bible." I was curious about why I was so often lost when "the Bible" was quoted in English, and I wanted to be able to follow the conversation. To do that, I had to read translations.

With two Christian translations on my shelf, I started to collect Jewish translations into English, beginning with the Jewish Publication Society's translation from 1985. Later still, I looked at earlier versions from the Jewish Publication Society, especially the 1917 translation, which is often far closer to the King James Version than is the 1985 edition.

As the project began to take months, and then years, I added even more voices: first the Jewish Study Bible, and then a red-letter Bible that highlighted what it considered to be the words of Jesus. I found the translation of Everett Fox, which makes an important effort to re-create the sound of Hebrew. The Fox translation is inspired, in part, by the work of Martin Buber and Franz Rosenzweig, who started translating the Hebrew Bible into German in 1925 while attempting to preserve the sound of Hebrew.

I began collecting all kinds of Bibles, in translations of varying quality. I accepted all offers of Bibles, and all recommendations; my neighbor in Iowa City, an evangelical pastor, lent me several Bibles and religious texts published by InterVarsity Press; my professor showed me an illustrated Bible dating to the nineteenth century. I picked up hotel Bibles and thrift store Bibles, and I walked through the Bible sections of bookstores when I traveled and bought the ones that looked interesting. One of my favorites, which I unfortunately later lost, was by a football coach who highlighted particular passages and explained how they related to the sport of life.

As the project grew, it followed me as I moved from Iowa City to San Francisco and back to the Midwest, to Iowa City again, to think and write in the quiet, and then to Chicago, where I now live. I also traveled to get a better sense of the Bible and its history. I flew to Geneva, Switzerland, where the International Museum of the Reformation has several sixteenth-century Bibles on display. My professor had told me many times to keep the Geneva Bible in mind as I read; the first full edition of the Geneva Bible, from 1560, had that same concept of text-plus-commentaries, text-plus-marginalia, as the *mikraot gedolot*. Walking around Geneva, through narrow brick passageways and squares full of bankers and well-dressed ladies, I thought about the Geneva aspect of the Bible's history and wondered how the Bible would be read today if the Geneva Bible had come to dominate the way future generations read. I imagined life with a Geneva Bible in hotel drawers, encouraging sleepless travelers to think of multiple meanings in their reading instead of just one firm meaning, a meaning as unshakable as insomnia.

THOSE TRAVELS GAVE ME AN appreciation for the physical element of a life of biblical commentary: it took time, and money, but also physical strength to continue. At times I found my own physical and mental energy waning as the project rolled on. The yellow legal pads on which I kept my notes felt heavy in my hands; the multiple Bibles sagged in my arms. I wondered why I was still bothering to take notes on every little moment that surprised me in English. I wondered if anyone who read English cared about Hebrew. At times I felt split in two. But I kept going so I could understand the two halves of my mind and my heart. It is the conversation I have been having with myself all my life: Hebrew, English, Hebrew, English. And I tried not to forget the tremendous sacrifice of time on the part of the translators and commentators—the donation of their own lives—as I read many translations that were far from perfect. I found myself thinking about how the different biblical commentators related to one another, and how there was a web of friendship and competition that crossed countries and centuries.

But I knew none of that when I started.

It took me years to figure out how to organize this project. Over time, I put my notes into various piles, and then rearranged the piles in an effort to catch the major differences between the Bible in Hebrew and the Bible in English. I transformed a linen closet into a manuscript closet, with shelves of notes; numerous drafts; maps of thousand-year-old Jewish neighborhoods in European cities; hand-drawn renderings of tiny towns that were important to medieval biblical commentators; and folders full of postcard images of buildings, churches, bridges, and city walls that were there during the years the commentators lived. I was constantly asked by friends and colleagues, and even people who passed me sitting with my tower of Bibles in coffee shops: "What's the difference between the Hebrew Bible and the English?" Of course, I wanted to give a short, clear answer, and I struggled to come up with an "elevator speech" explaining thousands of years of thought, argument, and discussion.

Most of the differences come down to grammar. English and Hebrew have different rules of sentence structure and divergent means of word structure, which is not that surprising, because Hebrew is a Semitic language and English is Indo-European. Beyond that, biblical Hebrew is ancient and modern English is only a few hundred years old.

The challenge of translating grammar, which often evaporates in translation, means that the Hebrew Bible and the English Bible differ in verse length, punctuation, and sound. The Bibles in each language depart further in how the names of men, women, and God are conveyed and what they mean, and in word choice and how repeated words do or do not carry additional weight. One verse might include all of these issues, making it very difficult to distinguish these "translation issues" into discrete categories. For those for whom grammar is a list of rules—charting verbs and memorizing exceptions—grammar might sound boring. My mother taught me that grammar is more than that; it is a window into how a group speaks to itself, structures its own thoughts, and defines its world.

Grammar might seem dull, but it is from the structures of the respective languages that everything else emerges. The differences affect so much, from how law comes across, to how characters are portrayed, to how the music of the Bible does or does not translate. This tends to influence how morality, history, and time are conveyed in each language—all essential stuff. At its base, however, these differences can be encapsulated in one word, "grammar," which affects everything. I therefore looked at how grammar affects key aspects of the Bible, including the story of creation, the depiction of love, the portrayal of God, and the introduction of man.

As MUCH AS THIS BOOK deals with issues of grammar and translation, and how syntax and word choice affect this extraordinary text, the Bible is a lived experience as well. I grew up living the concept of six days of work and one day of rest. It was and is so natural to me that I did not understand at first how much it influenced my reading. But eventually I realized I was not comfortable organizing my book only according to the rational issues of translation. That felt like part of the story, not the whole. It was essential to figure out a way to reflect the deep connection between text and time in the history of the Bible, and in readers' lives. The cyclical nature of the Jewish reading of the Bible is an intimate part of how the Hebrew Bible is experienced; each year, the Five Books of Moses are read aloud, week by week. Just as creation itself repeats in some way each week, with the return of work and the return of the Sabbath, so the constant quest to understand the Torah returns. It is a journey that goes around and continues, and it does not end, like time itself.

In this way, in my emphasis on the lived experience of the Bible and not just the read experience, I felt faithful to both my competing impulses. The first was to chronicle and explain surprises, to delineate the differences between the Hebrew and its English translation, as a teacher might; and the second was to make the Hebrew Bible, as it is read in houses like mine, alive to an English reader. My goal was, to the best of my ability, to re-create the conversation of home. This liveliness matters because the entire long story of the Hebrew Bible is, in part, about the tie between story and how to live, and quite plainly between reading and staying alive.

This is not something I alone feel. The Jewish liturgy emphasizes this idea. When the Torah scroll is put back in the ark after it is read, the entire synagogue sings the verse "It is a tree of life for those who take hold of it." Sometimes, listening to that verse, I think of how untrue it is: so many of the people who clung to the Torah in the past received anything but a long life. Sometimes that verse bothers me so much that I cannot sing it. But if "the language of the Torah" is substituted for "the Torah" itself, the verse is both true and untrue.

Hebrew was not spoken regularly for nearly two thousand years; as a spoken language, it was dead. But throughout the long exile that stretched from the Roman conquest of Jerusalem in 70 C.E. until the founding of the State of Israel in 1948, biblical Hebrew, what religious Jews call *lashon hakodesh*—literally, the holy tongue—was the preeminent language of Jewish scholarship and prayer. Over two thousand years, additional forms of Hebrew developed alongside biblical Hebrew, such as medieval Hebrew. Many of the most beautiful prayers are actually medieval poems, some written by rabbis with double lives as both poets and biblical commentators. Hebrew was also part of the various Jewish languages that developed in exile; the best-known are Yiddish, a thousand-year-old mix of German and Hebrew, and Ladino, or Judeo-Spanish, a mélange of Spanish, Hebrew, and Aramaic, with some Arabic, Turkish, and Greek influences, which developed after the expulsion of Jews from Spain in 1492. Then, about 130 years ago, despite the usual pattern of ancient languages evaporating along with their speakers, Hebrew began to revive as a spoken language. It is the only example in all of history of an unspoken language becoming a mother tongue again.

The revival began with one family, or, more precisely, with a determined man who decided to speak only Hebrew to his son. That father, a newspaper editor named Eliezer Ben Yehuda, also compiled the first modern Hebrew dictionary. Ben Yehuda had his own fascinating life story, including his study at the Sorbonne in Paris, his marriages to first one sister and then another, and his move, in 1881, to Ottoman-era Palestine, where he settled in Jerusalem. Without Ben Yehuda's determination, Hebrew might have continued to be a language of libraries, not kindergartens. Modern Hebrew, the language first spoken by the Ben Yehuda family, is rooted in ancient Hebrew, and many of its words and phrases come directly from the Bible. I imagine that the Ben Yehuda home was full of jokes, quotations, and vocabulary from the Torah, just like the house I grew up in. When they grabbed onto the ancient language and rooting family life in it, the lives of Ben Yehuda's son, of my parents and my siblings, and of so many other Hebrew speakers were invigorated. By basing speech in the far past, these new generations of Hebrew speakers created a deep sense of home.

MORE OFTEN THAN NOT, MY stories of translation are therefore told within the context of family and home. I know of no other way to write this space between languages, and the layers of meaning in individual ancient words, than to include the people and places of my early life. In my hometown in New York, major and minor rabbis disagreed in the streets, while in my home itself, my parents and siblings argued over the words of the Torah at the dining table.

But I had to venture far from the house I grew up in for this project. I did not realize that this was a well-worn path, to travel far in order to read, but I now know it is a very old story. To give you a sense of the multiple worlds and times in which I traveled, I offer some visual clues, including excerpts from the original Hebrew text, ancient and medieval commentaries, and English translations from several centuries.

In the back of this book, there are a few visuals that can help the reader track the long and fascinating story of the Bible, a history that is practically a grammar of its own. There is a chart of the Ten Commandments in Jewish, Protestant, and Catholic traditions, and a list of the books of the Bible according to Jewish, Protestant, and Catholic traditions. There is also a timeline of the major translations of and commentaries on the Bible, starting with the Septuagint, which was published a staggering twenty-two hundred years ago. Such information only reminded me how large the story of the Bible in translation is, and how small any effort to understand it must be.

The Bible's move to English was influenced by languages other than Hebrew, including Greek, Latin, Aramaic, and Arabic. This book focuses on the Hebrew-English aspect of the conversation, but I encourage readers to look into the story of the other languages as well, even if those stories do not seem relevant at first. It is illuminating to know that a Latin translation of a major Hebrew commentator had some influence on the 1611 King James Version in English, for example, just as it is fascinating to know that the tenth-century translation of the Bible from Hebrew into Arabic by Rabbi Sa'adiah ben Yosef al-Fayyūmi Gaon—generally referred to as Sa'adiah Gaon—was among the models for the 1985 Jewish Publication Society translation from Hebrew into English, published in America.

My hope is that these pages will spark discussion and ignite understanding. *The Grammar of God* is not a scholarly work but a personal one, a Hebrew speaker's response to the Bible in English. It is a book that, I now realize, after more than a decade of wrestling with these texts, I had to write—because nobody else can write how you view your home except you. The spark was the graduate school course I took, but the fire was the constant feeling that there is an ocean separating Hebrew and English, my two languages.

I also had to admit, as I waded deeper into this project, that

I learned more than language in the house I grew up in. Slowly, I understood that the way I read is intertwined with the way my family reads. Investigating the often tumultuous lives of the commentators, reading biographies and looking for patterns, I noticed that the idea of family influencing reading is actually a centuries-old phenomenon. The commentators' lives are also the stories of fathers and sons and even daughters. Rashi, who had no sons, famously taught his daughters, who became unusually learned; sometimes an older sibling, a grandparent, or a father-in-law was the first real teacher of a major scholar. The father of Maimonides was an extremely respected scholar in his own right, and probably his son's first important teacher; Maimonides' brother, David, who tragically died in a shipwreck, supported Maimonides financially until he was about thirty, opening a door to a scholar's life. Rashbam, a major commentator, and Rabbeinu Tam, an important rabbinical thinker, were the grandsons of the great eleventh-century commentator Rashi. Perhaps the commentaries of Rashbam and Rabbeinu Tam were in part the stories of grandsons, not just the record of scholarship.

These family ties—these connections of conversation and study and, yes, love—are essential not only in the lives of giants but also to the lives of ordinary readers. Once, as a journalist in Israel, I had the pleasure of listening to a lecture by a professor of poetry at an Israeli university. She had grown up in the former Soviet Union, where her grandmother had taught her the Psalms from memory, she said, with the windows closed and the blinds drawn and one ear always open for the authorities knocking at the door. It is impossible to tell the story of the Bible in Hebrew without including readers like that brave grandmother, who fought to make Hebrew central in a world that often wanted to shunt it aside.

The story of translation moves along an opposite path, one set into motion by the fear that Hebrew would soon be forgotten. The first major biblical translation, the Septuagint, was commissioned by the Jewish community of Alexandria, Egypt, because they were worried that future generations would not be able to read and understand the Torah in Hebrew. In fact they themselves may have already had limited or no knowledge of Hebrew; whether Philo (c. 20 B.C.E.–c. 50 C.E.) could read the Bible in Hebrew at all is a matter of scholarly dispute. It appears that Philo mainly used the Septuagint translation into Greek. I sometimes wonder if the Alexandrian Jews could imagine a reader like me, growing up with Hebrew in America. I was given the exact education the Alexandrian Jews thought was about to leave the earth forever—and perhaps already had.

But for the reader who, unlike me, is coming to the Torah late in life, there is a tradition of that as well. Rabbi Akiva, the major first-century rabbi, was a shepherd with little education when he began Torah study as an adult; according to one legend, he was forty. Onkelos, the Roman convert, seems to have come to the Torah late, too. My own father went to a Hebrew school in the South Bronx as a child, but like thousands of American Jews of his generation, he didn't truly learn Hebrew there. Instead, he became fascinated by Hebrew and Judaism relatively late, when he was about eighteen, in a slow and meandering process that involved a few books that entered his life in random ways, ranging from a prize my grandmother won, a textbook called *Ivrit Chaya*, or *Living Hebrew*, to a book of stories my aunt brought home, and coupled with the realization, from his college Russian classes, that a language could be learned. My father describes looking up the words of the Bible in a Hebrew-English dictionary, and then making his way to his first real Bible class, taught by a Conservative rabbi.

My father happened to walk in when the class was studying the story of Abraham; he was shocked and moved by the opening words of what in Jewish tradition is a section called Lech Lecha, or literally "Go, Go," the tale of a man going in an entirely new way, of a person following his own path. There is something cinematic about the story of Abraham, something bare and elemental that has swayed readers for generations. Both kinds of readers—the early-in-life readers and the late-in-life readers—continue to arrive on their own individual paths. Both groups of readers help inform the multilingual, multiperspective story of the Bible and its survival.

This story of a reader, and a family, of a book and a culture that is always in danger of dying out, is an offering to you, the reader of English, of a glimpse of the deep water of ancient Hebrew. More than anything else, this book is a call for conversation about how we read, and how we of the twenty-first century live with and live out those readings from centuries ago.

THE
GRAMMAR
OF GOD

CREATION

א בְּרֵאשִׁ֖ית בָּרָ֣א אֱלֹהִ֑ים אֵ֥ת הַשָּׁמַ֖יִם וְאֵ֥ת הָאָֽרֶץ׃

אונקלוס: א בְּקַדְמִין בְּרָא יְיָ יָת שְׁמַיָּא וְיָת אַרְעָא

תולדות אהרן: בראשית

רש"י

בראשית וגו' — אמר רבי יצחק לא היה צריך להתחיל את התורה אלא מהחודש הזה...

שפתי חכמים

א בראשית...

אבן עזרא

...חכמונו אמרו שהבי"ת נוסף כמו כבי"ת...

אבי עזר פי' על אבן עזרא

(א) חכמונו אמרו (שבס"ח נוסף וכו')...

רמב"ן

(א) בראשית ברא אלהים. אמר רבי יצחק לא היה צריך להתחיל התורה אלא מהחודש הזה...

ספורנו

(א) בראשית בתחלת הזמן והוא רגע ראשון בלתי מתחלק...

והארץ

בְּרֵאשִׁית
Bereishit
In/at the beginning

בָּרָא
bara
created

אֱלֹהִים
elohim
God

אֵת
et
[no English equivalent;
introduces a definite direct object]

הַשָּׁמַיִם
hashamayim
the skies; the
heavens

וְאֵת
ve'et
and et [see et above]

הָאָרֶץ
ha'aretz
the earth/land

וְהָאָרֶץ
V'ha'aretz
And the earth/land

הָיְתָה
hayta
was [feminine verb, past tense]

תֹהוּ וָבֹהוּ
to'hu va'vo'hu
wild emptiness; void

וְחשֶׁךְ
v'choshech
and darkness

[The phrase to'hu va'vo'hu appears only twice in the Bible; the other
place is Jeremiah 4:23.]

עַל־
al
on

פְּנֵי
p'nei
[the] face

תְהוֹם
t'hom
water; deep water

["Face" in Hebrew is always plural; the same is true for "water" and
"life."]

וְרוּחַ
veh'ruach
And the wind/spirit

אֱלֹהִים
elohim
[of] God

מְרַחֶפֶת	עַל	פְּנֵי	הַמָּיִם
merachefet	*al*	*p'nei*	*hamayim*
flutters/hovers	on	face	[of] the water

1 In the beginning God created the Heauen, and the Earth.
2 And the earth was without forme, and voyd, and darkenesse was
vpon the face of the deepe: and the Spirit of God mooued vpon the
face of the waters.

Genesis 1:1–2, King James Bible (1611)

1 When God began to create heaven and earth—
2 the earth being unformed and void, with darkness over the
surface of the deep and a wind from God sweeping over the
water—

Jewish Publication Society Bible (1985)

1 At the beginning of God's creating
of the heavens and the earth,
2 when the earth was wild and waste,
darkness over the face of Ocean,
rushing-spirit of God hovering over the face of the waters—

Schocken Bible (*The Five Books of Moses*,
translated by Everett Fox, 1997)

1 In the beginning, when God created the universe,
2 the earth was formless and desolate. The raging ocean that
covered everything was engulfed in total darkness, and the Spirit of
God was moving over the water.

Good News Bible–Today's English Version,
American Bible Society (2001)

1 In the beginning God created the heavens and the earth.
2 And the earth was waste and empty, and darkness was on the face of the deep, and the spirit of God was hovering over the face of the waters.

Darby Bible (1890)

1 When God began to create heaven and earth,
2 and the earth then was welter and waste and darkness over the deep and God's breath hovering over the waters,

Genesis: Translation and Commentary
(Translated by Robert Alter, 1997)

———◆———

M Y FAMILY GENERALLY DISCUSSES THE GRAMMAR OF CREATION when I'm carrying at least thirty pounds of food. I've often walked into the dining room with a heavy platter of chicken and roasted potatoes just when my brother brings up the first line of Genesis, the opening of the world.

"It's a problem," my younger brother Davi says. "Every commentator knows it's a problem."

"It all comes down to how you read that one word," my mother says. "Do you read the verb in the first line as *bara*, in the past tense, so that it means 'In the beginning God *created*,' or do you read it as *bro*, a form of the infinitive, so that it reads 'In the beginning of God's *creating*'?"

Someone reaches for the asparagus.

"*Bereishit bara elohim et hashamayim ve'et ha'aretz,*" Davi says. In the beginning God created the heavens and the earth. I can guess what he's thinking. If Genesis 1:1 says that God definitively created the heavens and the earth, over and done with, then why would line 2 go on about the time before the earth's creation, saying "and the earth was without form, and void" as if line 1 weren't even there?

I survey the table, looking for an empty spot to put the platter down. For the moment, everyone seems focused on eating. There are eight of us: my three younger brothers, my younger sister, my mother and father, and my grandmother—my father's mother—who lived with us then, and remained for more than a decade. I'm nineteen, my next brother, Amiad, is seventeen and a half, and Davi is sixteen. My sister, Merav, is twelve, and our youngest brother, Daniel, is six.

"Maybe the beginning isn't exactly the beginning," Davi says.

The Shabbat candles flicker desperately, as if they know their stay on earth is limited to this meal, their lives as short as a conversation.

Here we are again, on the seventh day, discussing the Hebrew of the first day.

"I remember reading Ramban in the eighth grade," Davi continues, referring to the thirteenth-century commentator who lived in Christian Spain. "And what he said about the first line of the Bible. I thought it sounded a lot like evolution, what we were learning about in the afternoon."

"That's ridiculous!" my father suddenly screams. "Don't be absurd!"

"Why?" Davi says.

Davi ducks out of the way as I lift the platter over his head in an effort to reach the empty spot of table space directly in front of him. And he gives me a look that says, Isn't there anywhere else you can put this?

Well, no. It's the only spot. And this table is, sometimes, the only place on earth where I can fight with myself and my family and God and the opening lines of the Bible all at the same time.

"I'm just saying," Davi continues, "Ramban's idea that everything was there, just formless, but was given form later is very close to what Darwin says hundreds of years later. Don't you think it's similar?"

"I can't even listen to this," my mathematician father says. My father has spent years of his life studying physics, battling math, and immersing himself in the history of discovery. The idea that Ramban's rambling comment even approaches Darwin's achievement infuriates him. "This is science. The rabbis—that's absurd!"

Davi recites what Ramban says anyway.

I sigh and settle in for a long discussion. Ramban's commentary on Genesis 1:1 happens to extend for pages. Ramban, also known as Nachmanides, often writes long entries, and he goes all out about the very beginning of the Bible. First, he insists that the idea that God created the world is the core of belief. But eventually he moves into radical territory by trying to understand why there is so much text about creation after Genesis 1:1, from the making of man to the Garden of Eden scene to the near-destruction of the world and the saving of Noah. And that's when things get interesting.

Ramban argues that what God created in Genesis 1:1 was a formlessness, which God later changes into form. In the beginning, Ramban suggests, God created primordial matter that later became the various parts and inhabitants of the world.

"Well, what if line one isn't the real beginning, anyway?" someone interrupts.

When this conversation erupts again a decade later, while I am a graduate student at Iowa, twenty-nine years old and home for the holidays, I smile to realize that at least this part of life has not changed.

As the discussion quickly moves to where the Bible should have started in the first place—Rashi, in his commentary on Genesis 1:1, quotes his father, Rabbi Yitzchak, who says the Torah should have begun with the first moment of nationhood, and not with creation—I think about how little of the rabbis' elaborate commentary could be elicited from the English translation. In the 1611 King James rendition of Genesis 1:1—"In the beginning God created the heavens and the earth"—there is no room for mystery. There is no room for puzzlement, no room for what prompted the rabbis' lengthy commentary.

Rashi reads Genesis 1:1 as a clause or a phrase connecting Genesis 1:1 and Genesis 1:2 into one long sentence. This reading is nothing like the King James Bible's two-sentence translation for Genesis 1:1–2, but it is pretty much how Genesis 1:1–2 comes across in the most recent Jewish Publication Society translation, published in 1985:

> When God began to create heaven and earth—the earth
> being unformed and void, with darkness over the surface of
> the deep and a wind from God sweeping over the water—
> God said, "Let there be light"; and there was light.

That "began to create" is close to what Rashi is trying to convey. Rashi believed that *bara*, the word frequently translated as "created" in Genesis 1:1, should be read as *bro*, a form of the infinitive, so that it reads 'In the beginning of God's creating,' the argument my mother was referring to.

But how, exactly, does Rashi come to this conclusion, and why is it so confusing to begin with?

The answer is one of my mother's all-time favorite dinner topics: vowels.

In Hebrew, vowels—dots and dashes located above, beneath, and inside letters—frequently determine meaning. And Rashi claims that in Genesis 1:1, the vowels should have been rendered differently. This complaint isn't unreasonable. In the medieval era, and in our own, typos and human errors were not unheard-of phenomena. Then as now, they can be both irritating and critical, prompting irate letters to the editor—and pages of biblical commentary, which is pretty much what Rashi is doing in his commentary on Genesis 1:1.

Rashi, in the eleventh century, can argue that the vowels are wrong because he knows that written vowels were added to the text only in the eighth century, and before that, the reading of the text was passed along orally, from teacher to student, parent to child, perhaps around tables like the one we are eating at right now. Rashi uses his deep knowledge of the text, of all that comes after Genesis 1:1, to help him, just as a modern reader might use past experience to flag a typo. In this case, Rashi thinks there should have been a dot above the verb instead of lines beneath it. It is the verb, and more specifically the grammatical state of it, that determines a world of meaning.

It's not just recent Jewish translations that are defining the verb in Genesis 1:1 as a phrase, as Rashi did. Interestingly, the New Oxford Annotated Bible, New Revised Standard Version, published in 2001, also combines Genesis 1:1 and 1:2. It reads:

In the beginning when God created the heavens and the earth, the earth was a formless void and darkness covered the face of the deep, while a wind from God swept over the face of the waters.

I look over at my father, who is eating peacefully again. Maybe my father is simply too hungry to comment on evolution. In previous meals, he has said something like "There is no way the rabbis knew about evolution. No way, or the entire history of science would be different!"

In the rare silence, I imagine the Shabbat meals of several hundred years ago, eaten by candlelight. When Ramban lived, evolution wasn't a dominant idea, though Aristotle had already suggested it. Perhaps the thirteenth-century concept of evolution was more like a few observations scribbled on a scientist's pad, like the calculations my father leaves around the house on yellow legal paper in his pursuit of a beautiful theory or what his field calls an "optimal experimental design."

I don't really know what "optimal experimental design" means, but to me what is optimal is the sight of work; I love seeing the start of creation. And I like that I can't even understand what I read in my father's neat handwriting. I see equations, x's and y's, the linearization of some polynomial—it doesn't matter. What is beautiful is the process of his thought, the fact that the questions go on, that my father is not troubled by not finding definite answers.

It's a little like some of the rambling moments in biblical commentary; what grips me is how the commentators get where they are going question by question, point by point, and how sometimes even the great Rashi writes *aineni yodeya*, which means, simply, "I don't know."

"All the commentators are interested in grammar," my mother says, moving the conversation back to her favorite subject while spearing a roasted potato. It is flavored with *chawaj*, a spice from the Arab world that finds its way into our chicken soup, too.

My youngest brother, Dani, and I try to look bored. My sister, Merav, who is seven years younger than I am, tries to focus on her plate, making her way through her vegetables with her usual efficiency. We have been listening to the grammar wars, the roar and explosion and finally the temporary calm, all our lives. But no amount of pleading can stop my mother from discussing grammar.

There is nothing more fascinating to my mother than the ways to look at an ancient word. For as long as I can remember, my mother has been trying to convince us that grammar is a universe, and that the tiniest parts of grammar tell a story. "It is impossible to read a word without its neighbors," my mother says to us. "You have to read the first line next to the rest."

The rest of us keep munching. Around us, the paintings on the dining room walls, all of them of Hebrew letters floating in the air, look on. They were once my grandfather's, painted by his rabbi and friend, a man as in love with the look of Hebrew letters as I have been with the conversation they create.

I GREW UP IN MONSEY, New York, a town twenty-five miles and a universe from Manhattan. Officially, Monsey is an unincorporated area, though a few years ago it was given a green-and-white sign on the highway. A few decades ago, Monsey was mostly farms and orchards, and there are still pear trees on the street where I grew up.

But in the Jewish world, Monsey is famous: it is sometimes called *ir hakodesh*, the holy city, the term usually reserved for Jerusalem, or *yerushalayim shel mata*, literally "the Jerusalem of below" or "the Jerusalem outside Israel." Monsey is home to thousands of rabbis, many students of the Torah, and important yeshivas—schools of Jewish higher learning. The word *yeshiva* comes from the verb *lashevet*, to sit or to settle, and many scholars seem to settle in for years, decades, even lifetimes. Some of the yeshivas belong to large, well-known Chassidic sects, like the Satmar or the Viznitz, whose yeshiva has castle-like towers. Chassidim are adherents of a movement that began in the eighteenth century, with the Ba'al Shem Tov—whose name literally means "bearer of a good name"—a rabbi who promoted the idea that emotions matter more than scholarship. This radical concept meant that a devout shoemaker could hold the same status as an erudite rabbinical student.

In addition to the major Chassidic sects that are represented in Monsey, there are smaller sects, like the Stoliner, whose school is on a main road; other sects' schools are not that easy to find. On the block I grew up on, there are Gerer Chassidim and Belz Chassidim, and not far away is the Popov Rebbe, a man I have heard of but never seen. These rabbis are major presences in the lives of their followers, and in Monsey. But as soon as I leave Monsey for Manhattan, or Newark Airport, the importance of the Popov Rebbe suddenly recedes. Still, the Popov Rebbe managed to have an effect on me. I once heard a conversation between two people who were trying to buy a house as close to the Rebbe as possible. Years later, when I tried to live as close as possible to writers I admired, I finally understood that aspect of what makes Monsey tick: the desire to live close to great teachers, to great thinkers, to the rabbinical presence.

You can reach Monsey from Manhattan on the Chassidic bus. With a curtain down the middle separating male and female riders, this was the bus I took to get to high school, and I often rushed on Friday afternoons to catch the last bus before Shabbat started, when I, like many other Monsey residents, would no longer be able to travel. On the bus, Yiddish is spoken—the thousand-year-old language of exile that is mostly a mix of German and Hebrew. All my life I have heard scholars lament the death of Yiddish at the hands of the Nazis, but I heard plenty of it in the streets and on the bus I took every day to and from school. Inside my house, though, we spoke Hebrew. Hebrew will always be my first language, the one I think in when I am tired, the one in which I first read and absorbed the Bible, the language of my dreams. English, however, is the language of my daily life, the language I work in and converse in with friends. There will never be a time when these two languages, and the cultures they represent, ancient and modern, will not be in conversation with each other in my head.

In Monsey many people spend the entire week preparing for Shabbat. The schedule for the neighborhood was more or less as follows: Monday might be the day for dry cleaning; Tuesday for laundry; Wednesday for the purchase of meat and the removal of household clutter; Thursday for the purchase of fish and fresh vegetables, the dusting of furniture and the polishing of silver and the baking of challah bread; Friday for the cooking of all the food. Some families were even more organized and began on Sunday, with everything cooked and ready to go by Thursday night.

We were Orthodox, a "modern" family, and by the time I was in junior high school the rest of the block was Chassidic. The Orthodox have their own network of schools, kosher stores, and fund-raisers, but the Chassidim were winning out on birthrate as well as Shabbat preparedness. Most of the Chassidim were ready for Shabbat by Friday morning. The women spent Friday sending the children out to collect charity for the less fortunate, showering, braiding and styling hair, and setting the table. Men went to the *mikvah*, the ritual bath. By late afternoon, the Polish maids were sent home. The workweek was over.

My family was different. Technically, the Hebrew word for people who are not Chassidim but who still keep the laws of the Torah is *misnagdim*—objectors. In the summer, we swam in pools with men and women—"mixed swimming," it was called. Scandalous, as was mixed dancing. My father, rebel that he was, mowed the lawn with his shirt off. There were other differences, other ways of objecting, or merely looking different, which in Monsey counted.

Though there were five kids in our house, plus a grandmother for a decade, by comparison our family was small. In all the years, through all the mess of eight people, we never had a maid, unlike the Chassidic families on the block with ten kids or more. We were also last-minute Shabbat preparers, and we tried to shop and clean and cook on Friday, which made that day crazy busy, always. My mother really couldn't devote six days a week to cleaning and cooking, and I don't think she ever wanted to.

Though she stayed home and took care of all of us full-time until I was thirteen, when she got a one-hour-a-day teaching job that paid for the bus I took to high school, she was always in school: graduate school, a world away in Manhattan. To the other mothers of the block, whose life was the home, my mother's travels to learn probably made her seem like a resident of a far-off galaxy.

My mother drove, whereas the other women did not, though she learned to drive fairly late, when I was thirteen and she was pregnant with my youngest brother. During the week she did not cover her hair, and on Shabbat she wore just a hat to shul, un-like the other married women, who wore wigs or kerchiefs called *ticheles.* And I'm sure the neighbors noticed her schedule: a light was always on in our house.

My mother had a life of the night. After everyone else went to sleep, she would sit at the dining room table with a large milkshake and several piles of dictionaries. She was reading Akkadian tablets—I know because I used to wake up at night and watch her, sitting in her nightgown with her very long hair pinned up, from the darkness of the kitchen. Piles of papers and pens before her, she'd talk to herself in some ancient language that she told me you could hear recorded at the Smithsonian Institution. From a room away, I heard the rhyme and rhythm of antiquity.

Sometimes, when I let her know I was awake by coming to the table, she would read me some Akkadian and translate it. She'd explain how it was so closely related to Hebrew and how it all rhymed. I thought that all mothers were like that—mothers in the daytime, and something secret between midnight and when everyone else woke up.

I still recall some of the Akkadian words: *imum*, mother, the word so like *ima*, the Hebrew word for mother. Then *abum*, the Akkadian word close to *abba*, the Aramaic—and modern Hebrew—word for father. *Kalbum*, dog, related to *kelev*, the Hebrew word.

The Akkadian stories were wild: tales of slaughter, of heads piled up. By the light of the dining room chandelier, my mother read me the Code of Hammurabi, a legal document dating from about 1780 B.C.E. And she laughed, not because of the horrifying punishments, but because the ancient—and all of its grammar— brought her joy.

My mother never finished her Ph.D., at Columbia University and the Jewish Theological Seminary, on an aspect of ancient syntax and the Bible. Her mentor died, and with five children, she could not easily relocate to another university in some other city. But she did continue learning, and teaching, and she instilled her love of the Bible, of Hebrew, of ancient language, and of language overall, into every one of her children. Though we have all loved language in individual ways, and though some of us have rebelled against it in our own ways, and though we have very different careers in law, business, translation, politics, and writing, we all have a fascination—or in some cases even an obsession—with it.

My mother did manage to carve out a teaching career. She has taught Hebrew at SUNY Rockland for twenty years and still enjoys packed classes and devoted students, but she is no ordinary Hebrew teacher. She teaches what is rooted in Ugaritic, Phoenician, Akkadian, Aramaic—all the languages she loves. A person who tries to learn Hebrew grammar from my mother learns the structure of antiquity, the building blocks of the ancient world. And though my brothers, my sister, and I are all grown, and no longer living in the red house in the middle of the big hill, I know my mother is still there, up late at night, reading ancient writing. The geography of her night has never changed: she's at the dining room table, in the chair just under the chandelier. Her books and her notebooks are lined up in front of her. The refrigerator behind my mother is buzzing, and in the freezer there is ice cream. If I close my eyes, I can hear the slurp of my mother drinking a milkshake in the relative quiet of the night.

I READ THE KING JAMES Bible out loud, sitting in my screened porch overlooking the backyard. It is my favorite place in Iowa City, a green refuge that is impossible to imagine from the front of the house, which faces a main road. In the back, the big weepy trees lean down; grapes climb the wooden fence next to the lone blueberry bush, just in front of the spot where raspberries grow wild and numerous in spring. The only noise is from the occasional rabbit searching for something to munch. A dirt road is visible just beyond the wooden fence, where I sometimes see my neighbor the pastor walking to the bus.

This afternoon, my other neighbor is working industriously on his lawn, leaving mounds of cut grass everywhere. All throughout our neighborhood in Iowa City is the sweet smell of freshly mowed grass. But I am also feeling industrious. The official text for my class is the Oxford Annotated Bible, but since the teacher repeatedly refers to the King James Version, I have decided to read that, too. And so I read aloud:

In the beginning God created the heavens and the earth.

I stop. There is a period at the end of the line.

A period!

All there is in the Hebrew is the *sof-pasuk*, two dots that come at the end of each verse, whether the verse is a sentence or a phrase, a statement or a question, a description or a command. The *sof-pasuk* reminds me of a line-ending in poetry; all it indicates is that a line ends there. But a line-ending in a poem is not a period.

Translating punctuation from the Hebrew Bible is a problem, since ancient Hebrew has no periods, commas, semicolons, colons, exclamation marks, question marks, or quotation marks.

The King James Bible, on the other hand, has a lot of punctuation. It affects tense, sound, and sense, but it also makes everything read slower. Way slower. With a period at the end of the sentence, God is definitely done with creation, instead of breathlessly rushing on and possibly still continuing. Staring at that period, I realize that my reading is stalling for an obvious reason: the King James Version is taking me longer to read because it *is* longer.

I read Genesis 1 out loud in both Hebrew and English. The English definitely has more words and syllables, but it also has more stops and starts. The breath required after a period simply adds time to the reading experience.

I DECIDE TO WALK THROUGH the King James Bible the way I was taught to walk through the Torah: I scrutinize every letter, every line break, every dot, every possible path. I leave the house and pass neat lawn after neat lawn, old, nicely painted home after old, nicely painted home, until I get to a line of new condos and then the cornfields. Walking by the tall stalks at the end of the road, I begin to count.

First I count letters. Then I count syllables, then words. The idea of counting as part of reading has been ingrained in me since elementary school; it is a standard part of education in yeshivas. As a child, I was taught that every letter in the Torah has a numerical value. *Aleph*, or *a*, has a value of one; *bet*, or *b*, has a value of two. There is an entire system, called *gematria*, based on the math of words—their value in numerical form—and the meaning that that number might lead to.

I recite the opening lines of Genesis in translation until it's obvious: English takes longer in every way.

Someone is honking.

"Are you all right?"

"Yes," I say. "I'm just counting."

The driver hurries away, but I continue to recite as I walk, slower than before. "In the beginning" is one word in Hebrew: *bereishit*. It's three syllables, and six letters. English, on the other hand, insists on three words, five syllables, fourteen letters just to get things going, just to convey the first word of the Bible. One, three, six, versus three, five, fourteen. It's somewhere between double and triple the length.

It's such a basic difference between languages, but it's a huge one.

ON THE WAY BACK HOME, I test out poems and stories I have memorized, with and without a period. There is a big difference between stopping and not necessarily stopping at key moments. Even at street corners there are crucial options: green light, yellow light, red light, a choice between a stop sign or no stop sign at all.

I sit in a coffee shop and email a dear poet friend for some outside-reader perspective on the first line of Genesis.

"What's the difference between a line-ending and a period?" I type.

The answer comes in less than a minute. Poets have priorities.

"The first is the end of a line of poetry," he fires back, "and the second is the end of a sentence in a poem. How does that grab you?"

Well, if a line that ends with no punctuation means a poem, then Genesis 1:1 is the start of a poem.

Is that even possible? Should I read the opening of the world as a poem?

No. Genesis 1:1, I reassure myself, is not a poem, no matter how it ends. It's just melodious prose. I've already spent hundreds

of hours of my life thinking about this verse, and now I'm supposed
to reframe it as a poem? Well, that doesn't grab me well at all.

"Ridiculous," I say to myself. But then I dismiss my hasty re-
jection of the idea. The whole point of reading the English translation is to consider other options, to see the entire world again.

In the beginning God created the heavens and the earth.

What could be more poetic than that, the sky and land rolling
out of nothingness? It's beautiful. My friend the talented poet is
absolutely right. Yes. Poetry.

No. Prose, I insist back, regaining my senses, remembering
the Hebrew. The line-endings of verses 1 and 2 don't rhyme.
They don't even have "slant rhyme," or similar-sounding endings that aren't exact rhymes but still give the listener some sense
of pairing. They don't share any similar sounds, the way lines of
ancient Hebrew poetry like the Psalms often do because masculine plurals generally rhyme with masculine plurals, while feminine plurals are another frequent source of rhyme. Instead, the
opening of the world puts *aretz*, earth (singular), with *shamayim*,
heaven (plural). They don't have a paired music, they don't echo
each other.

But my friend makes me realize that line-endings matter, and
that I have to pay attention to them as I make my way through the
translation. The way a line ends determines how the whole line is
read, in both languages. And in Genesis 1:1, this is the beginning
of the world: it's the line of all lines, the introduction of heaven
and earth. If it is ever reasonable to obsess about a single dot on a
page, this is the place.

That lone dot determines how a reader might see the world:
present, past, future.

* * *

BUT MAYBE IT'S NOT THE *look* of Genesis 1:1 and 1:2 that matters here, but the *sound* of it. In fact, all my life I have heard these lines, heard them more than seen them.

Maybe what matters is just how they sound out loud.

I decide to try this theory out on my poet friend: he is a person who breathes words and their rhythms, who understands sound.

"Do you always indicate a line-ending when you read it out loud?" I email, remembering that once, long ago, we sat through an entire class on the way Robert Frost worked with the sound of breath. Our teacher, in that class years ago in Boston, the great poet Derek Walcott, said that what distinguishes American poetry from poetry in other languages is the monosyllabic line, and that line requires that the writer figure out how to manipulate the act of breathing. Consider these two famous lines from Frost's "Death of the Hired Man," each word only one syllable:

Home is the place where, when you have to go there,
They have to take you in.

Even without the commas, it's clear that the speaker has to stop to breathe between "where" and "when" and between "there" and "they." The need to breathe is part of the music, and it also defines the meaning. It controls what is emphasized in this two-line span.

Frost, Walcott insisted, was a master of making breath, or the lack of it, part of his poetry. An example is Frost's opening line in the famous poem "Mending Wall":

Something there is that doesn't love a wall.

This classic line is built for an American speaker, with American intonations and patterns of breath. An American pronouncing this line would probably say: "Something there is" (breath, pause) and then recite "that doesn't love a wall" in one phrase, requiring no breath. That's because many Americans, speaking quickly—I remember Walcott demonstrating out of the side of his mouth—would connect "that" and "doesn't," so that the line would sound like:

Something there is thadoesn'tloveawall.

Frost understood how contractions in speech—like "doesn't"—help move one word into another, and the way some letters are swallowed by speakers of certain regions. He knew that "does not love a wall" would have an entirely different sound. Part of the power of Frost's line, I was taught, is the choice of the word "doesn't." "Doesn't love a wall" is one unit, one idea, one breath.

THIS IS THE STUFF I know my poet friend obsesses over, so I am pretty sure he will be open to devoting time to the exact way the ending of Genesis 1:1 sounds in English.

What I want to know is whether, if Genesis 1 is read as a poem, he thinks readers will stop at the end of line 1, separating verse 1 and verse 2 into two discrete units and therefore two stand-alone ideas.

"Well, of course people stop at least a tad," he replies in his Texas idiom, "at least mentally, at line endings, even if they are enjambments."

Of course? Just a tad?

I like the idea of enjambment, which is the running over of a phrase in a poem from one line into the next. It fits exactly with the ideas of Rashi, who reads lines 1 and 2 of Genesis together as one sentence. Interestingly, the Jewish Publication Society translation from 1985 doesn't just connect lines 1 and 2, as Rashi does, but also connects them with line 3, rendering the first three lines of the Bible as one long sentence:

> When God began to create heaven and earth—the earth
> being unformed and void, with darkness over the surface of
> the deep and a wind from God sweeping over the water—
> God said, "Let there be light"; and there was light.

Everett Fox also links verses 1, 2, and 3 in his translation, which sounds a little different. Fox is making a special—and impressive—effort to preserve some of the sound of the Hebrew. This can be heard in "wild and waste," which tries to mimic the Hebrew *to'hu va'vo'hu*, two mysterious words that have similar sounds and echo against each other:

> 1:1 At the beginning of God's creating of the heavens and
> the earth,
> 1:2 when the earth was wild and waste, darkness over the
> face of Ocean, rushing-spirit of God
> hovering over the face of the waters
> 1:3 God said: Let there be light! And there was light

My friend wants to say more, now that we've opened the subject of how to read the space—or non-space—between Genesis 1:1 and Genesis 1:2.

"I've been thinking more about this," he writes. He tells me that capitalization is also something to consider, that it, too, affects the way we rest and stop.

"Oh, no," I say out loud, and then hastily cover my mouth in embarrassment.

My fellow coffee drinkers look away. In this coffee shop, plenty of other writers have made the mistake of reading their work out loud to themselves—or worse, talking to themselves. I plan my response to my friend. I'll tell him there's no capitalization in Hebrew, in Genesis 1 or elsewhere. Capitalization makes everything look confident, definite, just as the period does: here, this is where it starts, this is where it ends. Capitalization helps close the door on doubt, just as the red letters in the Bible I recently bought try to make sure the reader knows exactly which phrases matter. It is one reason why the appearance of the Bible in Hebrew and English is dramatically different.

Later that night, unable to sleep, I write to my friend, "Genesis 1:1 is an open door."

He writes back: "Tell me more."

What should I tell him first, I wonder.

Genesis 1:1 is a microcosm of biblical Hebrew; it is ambiguous, rich, lyrical, evocative. But my friend and I are both in love with English, so I try to phrase it in terms of both languages. I try to think of how each language is built. Sentences in English tend to have a standard structure—subject, verb, object: but sometimes English, like most languages, is disobedient. A typically structured sentence in English might read, "Three girls walked into the store." But the classic John Updike story "A & P," written from the point of view of a young supermarket clerk, opens with the memorable sentence "In walks these three girls in nothing but bathing suits." That puts the verb phrase first, and of course it's not a grammatically perfect phrase—the girls are plural and should "walk," not "walks." There is also that famous and unforgettable opening line from Frost, which is also unusual in its word order: "Something there is that doesn't love a wall."

Hebrew is probably more flexible than English, especially biblical Hebrew: a sentence can begin with a subject, a verb, or an object. In the Hebrew Bible, a verb often appears before a noun; the common biblical phrase "and God said" is actually "and said God" in Hebrew, a construction not used in modern Hebrew. For translators, this one seemingly small difference in sentence structure can create big problems, because once the order of a sentence is altered, the meaning can be up for grabs, too.

Besides this difference in sentence structure, there is the additional complicated issue of word structure. Hebrew is a Semitic language, and therefore its words come from trilateral—that is, three-letter—roots. These roots can have multiple manifestations—as verbs, nouns, and occasionally even adjectives. These related words share a kernel of meaning, but it takes a somewhat knowledgeable reader to understand how a word functions grammatically in a particular passage. And that's not all. This root issue is exacerbated by the fact that the ancient text was not vocalized, or written out with vowels, until the eighth century. Furthermore, since, according to many scholars, the Bible was originally an oral composition, which was then copied and recopied by hand, human error—the tiniest slip of the hand—is certainly a possibility.

These three challenges—sentence structure, word structure, and centuries without an official version with all vowels included—led to errors of reading and translation. The infamous misreading of Moses as a creature with horns might be explained, in part, as an example of reading a verb as a noun. The Hebrew in

Exodus 34:29 beautifully describes Moses' skin as beaming with light; but some translators seem to have read the noun *keren*, which means both a ray of light and the horn of an animal, instead of the verb *karan*, "beamed." The words *karan* and *keren* share the same three letters, and therefore the same root (*krn*), but the lines and dots beneath the letters make them completely different words.

The "horned Moses" passage has its roots in St. Jerome's fourth-century translation of the Hebrew Bible into Latin, which became the official translation of the Catholic Church. Jerome's Latin version reads *cornuta esset facies sua ex consortio sermonis Dei*— "his face was horned from conversation with the Lord." Some scholars, who seemed unaware of this error in translation, argued that "horned" was actually an expression of authority and power. In time, Jerome's "horned" probably led to massacre—both noun and verb.

I was constantly reminded of the tremendous importance of verbs and their role in our understanding as I traveled through Europe trying to learn about the lives of the biblical commentators and finding myself looking up at church window after church window. In Hebrew, Moses is beaming; in Christian Europe, Moses is devilish, horned like an animal. If Moses could be transformed in translation, so could God. If human joy could be changed, so, too, could expressions of divine approval, or even divine love.

LOVE

תַּדְשֵׁ֤א הָאָ֙רֶץ֙ דֶּ֔שֶׁא עֵ֚שֶׂב מַזְרִ֣יעַ
זֶ֔רַע עֵ֣ץ פְּרִ֞י עֹ֤שֶׂה פְּרִי֙ לְמִינ֔וֹ אֲשֶׁ֥ר
זַרְעוֹ־ב֖וֹ עַל־הָאָ֑רֶץ וַֽיְהִי־כֵֽן:
יב וַתּוֹצֵ֨א הָאָ֜רֶץ דֶּ֠שֶׁא עֵ֣שֶׂב מַזְרִ֤יעַ
זֶ֙רַע֙ לְמִינֵ֔הוּ וְעֵ֧ץ עֹֽשֶׂה־פְּרִ֛י אֲשֶׁ֥ר
זַרְעוֹ־ב֖וֹ לְמִינֵ֑הוּ וַיַּ֥רְא אֱלֹהִ֖ים כִּי־
טֽוֹב:

תַּדְאֵ֣ית אַרְעָ֗א דִּתְאָ֤ה
עִשְׂבָּא֙ דְּבַ֣ר זַרְעֵ֔יהּ
מִזְדְּרַ֗ע אִילָ֤ן פֵּירִין֙ עָבֵ֣ד
פֵּירִ֔ין לִזְנ֕וֹהִי דִּי בַ֥ר זַרְעֵ֖יהּ
בֵּ֑יהּ עַ֣ל אַרְעָ֖א וַהֲוָ֥ה כֵֽן:
יב וְאַפֵּ֣יקַת אַרְעָ֗א דִּתְאָ֤ה
עִשְׂבָּא֙ דְּבַ֣ר זַרְעֵ֔יהּ
מִזְדְּרַ֤ע לִזְנ֙וֹהִי֙ וְאִילָ֤ן
עָבֵ֣ד פֵּירִ֔ין דִּי בַ֥ר זַרְעֵ֖יהּ
בֵּ֑יהּ לִזְנ֖וֹהִי וַחֲזָ֥א יְיָ֖ אֲרֵ֥י
טָֽב:

תולדות אהרן. למינו. חולין ס : ופתולא. חולין סס ר"ס ס"ו :

שפתי חכמים

נ ק"ל למה לא נא' תדשא הארץ דשא מזריע זרע או תעשיב הארץ
עשבים : ס י"ל דמזריע הוא ולשון מפעיל לשוה ספעיל לא הלשון...

רש"י

(יא) **תדשא הארץ דשא עשב.** לא דשא ל' עשב ולא עשב לשון דשא ולא
היה ל' המקרא לומר תעשיב הארץ שמיני דשאים מחולקין...

עץ פרי. שיהא טעם העץ כטעם הפרי והיא לא עשתה כן אלא ותוצא הארץ וגו'
ועץ עושה פרי ולא העץ פרי לפיכך כשנתקלל אדם על עונו נפקדה גם היא על עונה...

אשר זרעו בו. הן גרעיני כל פרי שמהן האילן צומח כשנוטעין אותו :
(יב) **ותוצא הארץ וגו'.**

רמב"ן

אלהים תדשא הארץ דשא. גזר שיהיה בתולדות
הארץ כח הצמחה וטולידי זרע כדי שיהיה המין קיים לעד...

אבן עזרא

הארץ ישראל. תולא. תולה. והנה שם כת בארץ ובמים לעשות
במצות השם זו וזו התולדות ועשב תדשא כמו תלמיד
אשר זרעו בו. שהזרע כפרי וכל א' שומר מינו :
ויאמר...

אור החיים

הכורא למינו. אלא לפן נשאו הדשאים ק"ו וכו'.
וקשה כי לסדר הכ' הקדים ה' דברים ה' לדשאים וה"ב...

ותוצא הארץ וגו'. אחר שאמר הכתוב ויהי כן לא היה צריך
לומר כל פסוק זה אלא הטעם היא להשמיענו ב' דברים...
וכא

וַתּוֹצֵא
Vatotzeh
And took out [feminine verb]
[See discussion of *vav hahipuch* on pages 38–39.]

הָאָרֶץ
ha'aretz
the earth/land [feminine noun]

דֶּשֶׁא
desheh
grass

עֵשֶׂב
esev
wild grass; weeds

מַזְרִיעַ
mazriah
[that] seeds
[masculine verb]

זֶרַע
zerah
seed [masculine noun]

לְמִינֵהוּ
l'minehu
of his kind

וְעֵץ
v'etz
and a tree
[masculine noun]

עֹשֶׂה־
oseh
[that] makes [masculine verb]

פְּרִי
pri
fruit [masculine noun]

אֲשֶׁר
asher
that

זַרְעוֹ
zar'oh
its seed [masculine noun]

בּוֹ
vo
[is] inside him

לְמִינֵהוּ
l'minehu
[to] his kind

וַיַּרְא
Vayahr
And he saw
[See discussion on page 39.]

אֱלֹהִים
elohim
God

כִּי	טוֹב
ki	**tov**
that [common conjunction in	good
Hebrew—can introduce narration	
and also indicate emphasis]	
וַיְהִי־	עֶרֶב
vayehi	**erev**
and there was	evening
וַיְהִי־	בֹקֶר
vayehi	**voker**
and there was	morning
יוֹם	שְׁלִישִׁי
yom	**shlishi**
day	third

12 And the earth brought foorth grasse, and herbe yeelding seed
after his kinde, and the tree yeelding fruit, whose seed was in it
selfe, after his kinde: **and God saw that** *it was* **good.**
13 And the euening and the morning were the third day.

Genesis 1:12–13, King James Bible (1611)

The earth brought forth vegetation: seed-bearing plants of every
kind, and trees of every kind bearing fruit with the seed in it.
And God saw that this was good. And there was evening, and
there was morning, a third day."

Jewish Publication Society Bible (1985)

12 So the earth produced all kinds of plants, **and God was pleased with what he saw**. 13 Evening passed and morning came—that was the third day.

> Good News Translation: Today's English Version
> (American Bible Society, 1992)

12 And the earth brought forth the bud of the herb, that seedeth seed according to his kind, also the tree that beareth fruit, which hath his seed in itself according to his kind: **and God**[a] **saw that it was good.**

13 So the evening and the morning were the third day.

Footnotes: a. Genesis 1:12 This sentence is so oft repeated, to signify that God made all his creatures to serve to his glory, and to the profit of man: but for sin they were accursed, yet to the elect, by Christ they are restored, and serve to their wealth.

> Geneva Bible (1599), reissued in 2006 by Tolle Lege Press

12 The earth produced vegetation: plants bearing seeds, each according to its own type, and trees bearing fruit with seeds, each according to its own type. ***Elohim* saw that they were good.**

13 There was evening, then morning—a third day.

> Names of God Bible (2011)

12 The earth brought forth sprouting-growth,
plants that seed forth seeds, after their kind,
trees that yield fruit, in which is their seed, after their kind.
God saw that it was good.

13 There was setting, there was dawning: third day.

> Schocken Bible (*The Five Books of Moses*,
> translated by Everett Fox, 1997)

WHEN I WAS FIVE YEARS OLD, MY NURSERY SCHOOL TEACHER got married. The entire school was invited to the wedding, and so we all got to see Morah Blimi (literally, "Teacher Blimi") arrive at the wedding hall with her hair uncovered, then leave the room briefly and return in a wig. I did not know it then, but beneath the wig, her head was entirely shaved. It was a Chassidic wedding, and so the festivities began with all the guests crying.

I had never been to a wedding before, and so I watched in awe as Morah Blimi's mother, female relatives, and friends—and Morah Blimi herself—all wept. Years later my mother explained the weeping to me. In Chassidic tradition, she said, a wedding is a leaving of the family of birth as well as a celebration. The most private part of a wedding, my mother was told by several Chassidic women, is what happens after all the guests leave. That's when the wedding poet arrives and sings a stanza of personal goodbye to each member of the bride's family.

Years later, as my sister plans her wedding, I keep thinking of that first wedding I ever attended, and I imagine the song I might write for my sister, if I knew how to do it. When I go home to Monsey, potential melodies are everywhere. Wedding music rocks the kosher supermarket, intrudes at the dentist's office, fills the Jewish bookstore. I notice how much weddings dominate life in the town we grew up in; they even reached Pathmark, the secular supermarket that has since closed, where prospective couples checked each other out in the parking lot. *Yes*, and a smile and a nod; or *no*, and the car doors slam. Now that wedding planning is our family's new topic of conversation, I notice the car doors opening, and closing, more clearly now, even though they have been there all my life. All the doors are reminding me that I have only a few weeks to go before my sister becomes a bride; if I want to come up with a gift of song, it had better be fast.

There is only one problem: I am slow.

At the post office, I notice that awards are posted for the massive volume handled by that particular post office in the past year—probably from all the wedding invitations, I'm thinking. Or maybe the award for volume got a boost from the large number of charity solicitations the community sends out, often in an effort to pay for weddings. The rest of the world may be phasing out snail mail; here, mail packs the bags of the postal carriers and stuffs the metal mailboxes of everyone who lives in town. It occurs to me that a wedding poet must have a regal role here, and an endless stream of business. For just a few minutes, the poet is the center of attention, just as, for one day, the bride.

For inspiration, I head to the most popular wedding hall in Monsey and look around. It is a Tuesday—the third day of creation, the day when "God saw that it was good" twice, according to Genesis. It is the day that many believe received a double dose of divine approval, or perhaps divine love, which is why it has long been the preferred day of the week to get married.

IN THE SCHOCKEN BIBLE TRANSLATION by Everett Fox, the double refrain of the third day of creation is apparent, as it is in most translations. Here is Fox's rendering:

9 God said: Let the waters under the heavens be gathered to one place, and let the dry land be seen! It was so.

10 God called the dry land: Earth! and the gathering of the
waters he called: Seas! **God saw that it was good.**
11 God said: Let the earth sprout forth with sprouting-
growth, plants that seed forth seeds, fruit trees that yield
fruit, after their kind, (and) in which is their seed, upon the
earth! It was so.
12 The earth brought forth sprouting-growth,
plants that seed forth seeds, after their kind,
trees that yield fruit, in which is their seed, after their kind.
God saw that it was good.
13 There was setting, there was dawning: third day.

I look out the car window. The parking lot in front of the
Atrium wedding hall just beyond Pathmark is packed. In Monsey,
there are always weddings on Tuesdays. Unfortunately, visiting
the parking lot does not yield a wedding poem for me. But I know
I want something of a double blessing for my sister, so I grab the
Hebrew Bible and the King James Version and find a place to sit
and write. It's a doughnut shop that's crammed with immigrants—
I hear Chinese and Spanish—and it reminds me of being in a new
country, which is what the early days of creation must have felt
like, to man and perhaps even to God. The woman who runs the
place says "Two?" constantly, in her effort to get everyone to buy
two doughnuts. As she keeps saying "two" I think again of God's
double approval of Tuesdays, and how clear it is in the Schocken
translation. I open the King James Bible and stare at the same line:

and God saw that *it was* good.

Throughout the King James Bible, words that have been added
from the Hebrew are italicized. In this case, the verb "to be" in

Hebrew is implied rather than stated when used in the present tense. I sit and stare at the two words for a little too long. Something is bothering me. What I am seeing is not what is. I read the section again: "And God called the dry land Earth; and the gathering together of the waters he called the Seas: and God saw that *it was* good."

I see now what I did not notice in the Everett Fox translation. A literal, word-for-word version of the Hebrew does not include the word "it." Instead, there is the little Hebrew word *ki*. "And God saw **ki** good." The Hebrew word *ki* is a challenge to translate; in modern Hebrew, it means "because," but "and God saw because good" doesn't feel quite right either. *Ki* in the Bible sometimes feels a little more like emphasis. What the King James translators have employed is both the simplicity and the certainty of the word "that." But *ki* feels different from "that"—it's both more complex and more elegant.

I open the Jewish Publication Society's most recent translation, from 1985, and see that it has "And God saw that **this was** good." "This" is a bit more emphatic than "it," but I'm still not satisfied.

Fortunately, my parents' library offers some other ideas. *Notes on the New Translation of the Torah*, edited by Harry M. Orlinsky and published in 1969, gives an inside look at some of the arguments and problems the Jewish Publication Society committee encountered in its effort to translate. It turns out that the word *ki* was one of the committee's problems. "The wide range of meanings commanded by the common conjunction *ki* has not been exploited fully in the traditional translations," the committee writes in the introduction. It quotes the Brown-Driver-Briggs *Hebrew and English Lexicon*, which explains "that *ki* often introduces the direct narration . . . in which case it cannot be represented in

English (except by inverted commas)." The committee notes that older translations had a different take on the word, which became "verily" and "certainly" at points in the 1917 translations.

Then, at the end of the page-long discussion of a simple conjunction, the committee delights me when it mentions that *ki* is a topic that can be talked about at length, and also that it can be used to emphasize. "Finally—since our word lends itself to almost limitless discussion in detail—the emphatic force of *ki* has often gone unrecognized, e.g. in Exodus 2.2, where NJV has 'and when she saw how [*ki*] beautiful he was,' where the older version read, 'and when she saw him that [*ki*] was a goodly child.'"

There appear to be two approaches to translating *ki:* understated and elaborate. Then the committee admits that "sometimes it is difficult to decide between the two; thus, earlier printings read '(God saw) how [*ki*] good this was,' . . . but this was given up in favor of the traditional 'that this was good.'"

I return to the Hebrew of the third day, and now what jumps out at me is one letter—the letter *vav* in the word *vayahr,* "and he saw." What it is doing in translation is not exactly what it does in Hebrew.

It may be difficult for a reader of English to imagine the significance of the word "and" in the famous refrain of creation, *vayahr elohim ki tov,* usually translated as "and God saw that it was good." In English, "and" is indicated by a word in its own right; in Hebrew it is indicated by a lone letter (a *vav*) attached to the word that follows it.

But it is no ordinary letter. Whereas in English "and" simply connects ideas or objects or actions, in Hebrew the letter *vav* can change the tense of the verb that follows it. For this reason, it is known as the *vav hahipuch,* the *vav* that turns over. In Hebrew, *vayahr,* "and he saw," begins with this particular *vav.* Its construction is an unusual mixture of past and future: *yireh*, "he will see," with a *vav* tacked onto it becomes a verb in the past tense. The resulting verb, *vayahr*, lives in a special zone of biblical time, a past tense that lies on the foundation of a verb in the future tense. Its sense of time reminds me of the centuries-old rabbinic discussion on the timing of creation. Perhaps this is why the verb strikes some Hebrew commentators as referring to something richer than literal sight. Ibn Ezra, the twelfth-century commentator, says "and he saw" means "in his thought." Ramban, or Nachmanides, from the thirteenth century, reads it as "thought in his heart." Rashi sees the word as both literal and metaphorical. Commenting on Genesis 1:4, the first appearance of the verb *vayahr*, "and he saw," in the Bible, when God "sees" that the light is good, Rashi quotes a story in which God decides that it's not good for the wicked to use the light, and therefore God separates it for the righteous to use in the future. Rashi writes that God sees that it is not desirable for light and darkness to be mixed together, and so God assigns light to day and darkness to night. All three medieval commentators, writing in different countries and centuries, read sight as more than just visual; for all of them, divine sight has an element of knowing. To see means to know, and perhaps to understand.

WHAT "SIGHT" MEANS MATTERS BECAUSE many of the Bible's plot twists involve sight—or perhaps some kind of knowledge. The first woman, Eve, "sees" that the fruit of the Tree of Knowledge is good to eat. Very quickly, Eve takes the fruit, and both she and Adam eat it. The power of looking and not looking, and knowledge and the lack thereof, are connected. Caught eating, Adam vainly tries to hide from God's sight. Caught murdering, Adam's son Cain tries to hide from God's sight, too. Later, Lot's wife famously turns back to take a last look at her old home, which she had been forbidden to do, and becomes salt. And God sees, too, in a way that often implies judgment. After creation, God sees that it is good, but here, God's sight is powerful and wide—and also frightening.

These sight-related episodes often involve ignoring an explicit spoken request God has made of man. These simple errors, the Bible tells us—as it delineates the pain Eve will endure in childbirth and the sweat Adam will experience as he works the earth—cause struggle to this day. But in Hebrew, they are perhaps even more chilling to read on the page.

Why?

In Hebrew, the words for "fear" and "sight" are visually close, and sometimes their verb forms actually contain the same letters. "To fear" has the three-letter root *yud, reish, aleph,* and "to see" has the three-letter root *reish, aleph, hey.* Because they do not share the same root, the concepts of sight and fear are not related in meaning. And yet, in certain biblical moments, in certain verb forms, sight and fear *look* identical—written with the same letters. Only their vowels distinguish them.

This occasional visual closeness of sight and fear in biblical Hebrew is impossible to see in English, but I wish there were some way to hint at it, to add a comment, to insert an asterisk, as so many readers have done for thousands of years. In the moments when "sight" and "fear" skid close to each other, in the moments when the verbs are written with identical letters, I think about how what we first see with our eyes is often quite far from what truly is—both in reading and in life.

I think, too, about the *look* of a story. For centuries, the Bible was an aural experience, a text read out loud, in public. It still is read out loud today. But today, when printed books are relatively affordable, and when online access makes reading the Bible entirely free, the ancient Bible is a visual experience as well as a heard one. What we see, or think we see, matters more than ever. And there is something potentially frightening about mistaking looking at God with fearing God—even if it's easy to see how that mistake happens.

The only cure for a quick glance is context. This is what so many of the rabbinic commentators try to provide—a map of how to read a verse within a neighborhood of other verses. It is as if the rabbis were creating a web of hyperlinks, encouraging the reader to read more, to see what other verses and ideas lie just beyond the boundaries of that particular page. The reader's task is not to be lulled by the promise of the familiar, not to simply accept a refrain as seemingly clear as the cheerful "and God saw that it was good."

The reader's task is to ask what is going on. No matter how many readers have read before him, the reader must read again, must investigate, must lift the veil to seek the face of the text, over and over again.

I FIND, TO MY DELIGHT, that the rabbis and translators obsess, as I do, over the little details that make up the first Tuesday. In line 12, the word for "grass," *desheh*, is right next to a word that, in modern Hebrew at least, is a synonym for "grass," *esev*—though it can also mean "weeds." The Oxford Annotated Bible translates the word as "plants," while the King James chooses "herbs." Interestingly, some of the commentators endorse both of these translations. Ramban, or Nachmanides, the thirteenth-century commentator, explains that there are two parts of the same plant—*desheh* and *esev*. The lower part of the plant, *desheh*, what is translated as "grass," grows close to the ground, but *esev*, the word that follows it, is large and seedful. *Esev* is the taller part of the plant, which produces seeds and thus makes reproduction possible. The wind can easily blow the seeds from *esev* all over the world.

If this sounds like over-obsession with detail, the rabbis don't seem to think that this emphasis on different types of vegetation is frivolous at all. Sforno, the Italian rabbi, commentator, and physician who lived from 1475 to 1550, explains that *desheh*, or "grass," is for animals to eat, and he gives a quote from the Book of Joel to back this up, whereas *esev mazria zerah*, the seedful part of the plant, is for humans to eat. As for what is often translated as "the tree yielding fruit," that, too, Sforno tries to explain: what is made from two types does not give birth. As usual, I think as I read, Genesis is about what will lead to what, what will give birth to what. God makes grass and animals and humans and then they all create in turn. Reading the English, I miss the alliterative sound of *tadsheh desheh:* "let grass grow," it says. The rabbis frequently point out that what is repeated in the Bible is significant. So why was the third day blessed twice? Why is any one day blessed more than the others?

Naturally, the rabbis discuss this. It's not that the third was better, Ramban, or Nachmanides, says, in a comment full of quotes from other rabbis who preceded him, but rather that there was no goodness on Monday. This is something plenty of modern office workers would agree with, but Ramban is simply counting, not expressing a desire for a life of leisure. Because "God saw that it was good" was left out on Monday, when Tuesday came, there was a need for two.

Then there is the Musaf Rashi, a commentary that literally means "an addition to Rashi." On the phrase *tadsheh desheh*, "let grass grow," this commentator adds: "Let her cover herself and dress herself in grass." The "her" is not a bride, but the earth. What interests me is this: bride or earth, the exalted being here is female.

The third day in Hebrew seems to have a feminine lilt to it. This is another element I find strange when reading the King James Version. Hebrew is a gendered language, and all nouns are either masculine or feminine. Not so in English, in which a table or a tree is neither masculine nor feminine. Yet on the third day the King James translation feels aggressively male.

Here is line 12 in the King James Bible:

And the earth brought foorth grasse, and herbe yeelding
seed after **his** kinde, and the tree yeelding fruit, whose
seed was in it selfe, after **his** kinde: and God saw that it was
good.

In Hebrew, *aretz*, "earth," is feminine, so what is translated as "brought forth"—*vatotzeh*—is a feminine verb in Hebrew. And while the grass—what is translated as "herb-yielding seed"—and the tree are both masculine nouns in Hebrew, the reader of English may not realize that even if the trees and the grass are male, the earth itself, to which they belong, is female.

The Hebrew commentators, who mostly predate the King James Bible and the rise of English, do not comment on the fact that "earth" is a feminine noun; in a gendered language like Hebrew, it's not a major point. Yet when the rabbis focus on the numerous words for grass, even calling the grassing of the earth a *dressing* of the earth, they are referring to the festive feeling of the third day, the extra love given to it, and perhaps even the femininity of it. On the third day, after all, the bareness was covered.

My sister tells me that underneath the chuppah, the bridal

canopy, shoulders will have to be covered for everyone in the wedding party, the standard for religious weddings. It strikes me, as my sister discusses shawls and jackets, that the rabbis effusing over Genesis 1:12–13 had a point. There is something festive about being so dressed, something that is hopeful for the future— even though the rabbis meant the earth and not a bride. And then another aspect of the festivity hits me. God does not *say* that all that God created on the third day is good: instead, God *sees* it.

So much of creation is spoken—from "let there be light" to "it is not good for man to be alone." And yet, when it comes to approving the greening of the earth, there is not a word. God's famous double approval of the third day comes entirely without speech. *Syag l'chochma sh'tika*, the rabbis say. It is a comment perhaps appropriate to this moment of divine approval or divine love. It means: a guardian of wisdom is silence.

LAUGHTER

וְהִנֵּה־בֶן לְשָׂרָה אִשְׁתֶּךָ וְשָׂרָה שֹׁמַעַת פֶּתַח הָאֹהֶל וְהוּא אַחֲרָיו: יא וְאַבְרָהָם וְשָׂרָה זְקֵנִים בָּאִים בַּיָּמִים חָדַל לִהְיוֹת לְשָׂרָה אֹרַח כַּנָּשִׁים: יב וַתִּצְחַק שָׂרָה בְּקִרְבָּהּ לֵאמֹר אַחֲרֵי בְלֹתִי הָיְתָה־לִּי עֶדְנָה וַאדֹנִי זָקֵן: יג וַיֹּאמֶר יְהוָה אֶל־אַבְרָהָם לָמָּה זֶּה צָחֲקָה שָׂרָה לֵאמֹר הַאַף אֻמְנָם אֵלֵד וַאֲנִי זָקַנְתִּי:

אונקלוס

קַיְמִין וְהָא בַר לְשָׂרָה אִתְּתָךְ וְשָׂרָה שְׁמַעַת בִּתְרַע מַשְׁכְּנָא וְהוּא אֲחוֹרוֹהִי: יא וְאַבְרָהָם וְשָׂרָה סִיבוּ עָאלוּ בְּיוֹמִין פְּסַק מִלְמֶהֱוֵי לְשָׂרָה אֹרַח כִּנְשַׁיָּא: יב וְחַיְּכַת שָׂרָה בִּמְעָהָא לְמֵימַר בָּתַר דְּסֵיבִית תְּהֵי לִי עוּלֵימוּ וְרִבּוֹנִי סִיב: יג וַאֲמַר יְיָ לְאַבְרָהָם לְמָא דְנַן חַיְּכַת שָׂרָה לְמֵימַר הַבְרַם בְּקוּשְׁטָא אֵילִיד וַאֲנָא סֵיבִית:

תו"א ומלת מגילה ט מליאל מ. אחרי יופל פנ מליאל שם. ואחרי זקן יבמות שם.

שפתי חכמים

[dense commentary text]

רש"י

שֶׁל מָקוֹם הֵם אָ"ל כְּמוֹ וְיֹאמֶר לָהּ הַמַּלְאָךְ ה' הַרְבָּה אַרְבָּה וְהוּא אֵין בְּיָדוֹ לְהַרְבּוֹת אֶלָּא בִּשְׁלִיחוּתוֹ שֶׁל מָקוֹם אַף כָּאן בִּשְׁלִיחוּתוֹ שֶׁל מָקוֹם אָ"ל כֵּן (ב"ר). (אֱלִישָׁע אָמַר לַשּׁוּנַמִּית לַמּוֹעֵד הַזֶּה כָּעֵת חַיָּה מְחֻבֶּקֶת בֵּן וְתֹאמַר אַל אֲדֹנִי אִישׁ הָאֱלֹהִים אַל תְּכַזֵּב בְּשִׁפְחָתֶךָ. **אוֹתָן הַמַּלְאָכִים שֶׁבִּשְּׂרוּ אֶת שָׂרָה אָמְרוּ לַמּוֹעֵד אָשׁוּב אָמַר לָהּ אֱלִישָׁע אוֹתָן הַמַּלְאָכִים שֶׁהֵם חַיִּים וְקַיָּמִים לְעוֹלָם אָמְרוּ מֵת בֵּין חַי וּבֵין מֵת לַמּוֹעֵד הַזֶּה וְגוּ'):** **וְהוּא אַחֲרָיו.** הַפֶּתַח הָיָה אַחַר הַמַּלְאָךְ: (יא) **חָדַל לִהְיוֹת.** פָּסַק מִמֶּנָּה: **אֹרַח כַּנָּשִׁים.** אֹרַח נִדּוּת: (יב) **בְּקִרְבָּהּ.** מִסְתַּכֶּלֶת בְּמֵעֶיהָ וְאוֹמְרָה אֶפְשָׁר הַקְּרָבַיִם הַלָּלוּ טְעוּנִין וְלַד הַשָּׁדַיִם הַלָּלוּ מוֹשְׁכִין חָלָב תְּנוּבִּימִית: **עֶדְנָה.** צַחְצוּחַ בָּשָׂר וְל' מִשְׁנָה מֵסִיר אֶת הַשֵּׂעָר וּמַעֲדֵן אֶת הַבָּשָׂר. ד"אָ ל' עִדָּן זְמַן וֶסֶת נִדּוּת: (יג) **הַאַף אֻמְנָם.** הֲגַם אֱמֶת אֵלֵד: **וַאֲנִי זָקַנְתִּי.** שִׁנָּה הַכָּתוּב מִפְּנֵי הַשָּׁלוֹם

אבן עזרא

הָאַחֶרֶת וְשָׂרָה מֵיָה כְּמוֹ כֹּה לְחַי וְהוּא אַחֲרָיו. זֶה הַמַּלְאָךְ הַמְדַבֵּר עִם אַבְרָהָם הִי' אַחֲרֵי הָאֹהֶל וְאַבְרָהָם יוֹשֵׁב בִּפְתַח הָאֹהֶל וְגַם וְלֹא נִרְאָה שָׂרָה וְיֵשׁ אוֹמְרִים פֶּתַח הָאֹהֶל שָׂלֹה הָיָה אַחֲרֵי אֹהֶל אַבְרָהָם: (יא) **בָּאִים בַּיָּמִים.** הִגִּיעוּ לִימֵי זִקְנָה רַבִּים: (יב) **הָיְתָה לִי.** כְּמוֹ תִּהְיֶה לִי: **עֶדְנָה.** כְּמוֹ עֶדְנָה כְּמוֹ עֵדֶן וְעוֹנַג וְכֵן וּמִתְעֲדְנוּ. וְהַטַּעַם אַחֲרֵי שֶׁבָּלֹתִי וְזָקַנְתִּי אֵיךְ תִּתְחַדֵּשׁ לִי עֶדֶן וְעוֹנַג הַכְּעֹל. וְהַטַּעַם אַחֲרֵי שֶׁכְּבָר הָיָה בְּקִרְבָּהּ כִּנְכֶפֶשׂ וּשָׁם גָּלָה סוֹדוֹ לִמְלָאֵךְ: (יג) **וַאֲנִי זָקֵן.** פֵּרוּשׁוֹ וַאֲנִי זָקַנְתִּי בִּלְתִּי וְהַמַּלְאָךְ אָמַר אֱמֶת. וּמ"ס אָמְנָם נוֹסָף כְּמ"ס שָׁלֵם וּמְפָרְשִׁים אֲחֵרִים אָמְרוּ כִּי אֵלּוּ ג' אֲנָשִׁים נְבִיאִים הָיוּ. וְאִם שָׁעַן שְׁעוֹן הַלֵּב אַבְרָהָם נְבִיא אֵיךְ הָיָה וְאֵיךְ ל"א נָבִיא אֵל כִּי רַק אִם הָיָה גָּדוֹל מִמֶּנּוּ כִּנְכָלִים כַּמִּיִם וְהַבֹּרֵא. וְתַכְתָּב שֶׁלֹּא בָּאוּ לְאַבְרָהָם רַק לְשָׂרָה. וְכֵן אָמְרוּ אֵיךְ שָׂרָה אֶשְׁקָ וְהַשֵּׁנִים

רמב"ן

שִׁישׁוּב אֵלָיו אֶלָּא בִּשְׁלִיחוּתוֹ שֶׁל מָקוֹם אָמַר לוֹ כְּמוֹ וַיֹּאמֶר לָהּ הַמַּלְאָךְ ה' אָמַר אַרְבָּה אֶת זַרְעֵךְ וְהוּא אֵין בְּיָדוֹ לְהַרְבּוֹת אֶלָּא בִּשְׁלִיחוּתוֹ שֶׁל מָקוֹם אָמַר לוֹ אַף כָּאן כִּי מִפְּנֵי שֶׁהַקָּבָּ"ה הוּא אָמַר לוֹ בְּבֹאוֹ לְמוֹעֵד אֲשֶׁר אֲלֵיכֶן בַּמַּלְאָךְ אוֹ בְּהַקָּבָּ"ה לֹא מַצִּינוּ שֶׁבָּא אֵלָיו לְמֵימֵרָא אֵלָי נָכֹל ל' בְּלָשׁוֹן ה"א פָּקַד אֶת אַבְרָהָם וַהוּא כַּאֲשֶׁר אָמַר וַיֹּרֶשׁ ה' לְשָׂרָה כַּאֲשֶׁר דִּבֵּר וַה"א אֲשֶׁר בְּיוֹ וַיֹּאמֶר ה' אֶל אַבְרָהָם הוּא מְדַבֵּר הַמַּלְאָךְ בְּשֵׁם שֻׁלְחוֹ וְשָׁב אֵלָיו לְמוֹעֵד אֲשֶׁר דִּבֵּר אֹתוֹ וְאִם וְאָם לֹא בָא נִכְתָּב. וְהַנְכוֹן בְּעֵינַי שֶׁהוּא בֶּן חַיִּים וַיְהִיוֹת בֶּן לְשָׂרָה אֲשֶׁר שָׁאֲתָךְ חָזוּ כַּאֲשֶׁר נֶאֱמָר לְאַבְרָהָם לְמוֹעֵד חֹזַת בַּשָּׁנָה הָאַחֶרֶת יִחְיֶה אָשׁוּב כְּמוֹ רשב ח' אֱלֹהֶיךָ. **רְשָׁב וְקִצְבָּךְ: (יא) בָּאִים בַּיָּמִים.** וְהָאָדָם בִּימֵי בַּחֲרוּתוֹ יִקְרָא עוֹמֵד בַּיָּמִים וְיִקְרָאוּ יְמֵי רַק זִקְנָה וְיִחְיוֹת וְיָמִים רַבִּים מֵרוֹב בְּנֵי הָאָדָם בְּרוּרוֹ יִקְרָא יְמֵי בָּא מֵי מִפְּנֵי שֶׁהוּא כְּבָא בְּאֶרֶץ אֲחֶרֶת נֹסֵעַ מֵעִיר אֶל עִיר מִיּוֹם אֶל יוֹם: **חָדַל לִהְיוֹת.** הַפְּסֵק הָאָרֶץ מֵחֹמֶת וְזִקְנָה לְאַחֲרֵינָה: (יג) **וַאֲנִי זָקַנְתִּי.** הוּא פֵּרוּשׁוֹ אֲחֵרֵי בְּלֹתִי וְדִבְרָיו אֱמֶת אַךְ מִפְּנֵי הַשָּׁלוֹם

ספורנו

בְּפֶשַׁע: **וְהוּא אַחֲרָיו.** הַפֶּתַח שֶׁהִתְוַדַּע שָׁם שָׂרָה תַּשׁוּמַעַת הַמְדַבֵּר אֵלָיו כִּי זֶה הָרְבָּה וְחָשְׁבָה הַמַּלְאָךְ הַמְדַבֵּר לְפִיכָךְ לֹא דִבֵּר עִמָּהּ לֹנַכַח כְּמוֹ שֶׁעָשָׂה שֶׁלֹּא יוֹשֵׁב זֶה בּוֹקְנִים בַּבְּרָכָה שׁוּם נָבִיא כִּי אָמְנָם לַחֲשׁוֹב לְהַבְחָרָהּ אַחֵר חוּקְנָה חֲרִי הוּא כְּתִיּוּת מַחְמַת שֶׁלֹּא תְּהֵיֶה זִלְזוּל בְּמִצְוַת הָאֵל **אֱלִישָׁע: (יב) וַתִּצְחַק שָׂרָה.** שֶׁחֲשָׁבָה שֶׁהָיָה דָבָר הַמַּלְאָךְ בְּרָכַת

וְאַבְרָהָם
V'Avraham
And Abraham

וְשָׂרָה
v'Sarah
and Sarah

זְקֵנִים
zekainim
[are] old [plural]

בָּאִים
bah'eem
coming
[Figuratively, "coming in days" = old]

בַּיָּמִים
bayamim
in days

חָדַל
chadal
had stopped

לִהְיוֹת
l'hiyot
to be

לְשָׂרָה
l'Sarah
for Sarah

אֹרַח
orach
the way

כַּנָּשִׁים
ka'nashim
of/like women

וַתִּצְחַק
Va'titzchak
And she laughed

שָׂרָה
Sarah
Sarah

בְּקִרְבָּהּ
be'kirba
inside her; in her gut

לֵאמֹר
leimohr
to say

אַחֲרֵי
acharei
after

בְלֹתִי
v'loti
[me being] worn out
[Figuratively, "I have been
old"]

הָיְתָה־
hayta
there was

לִּי
li
for me

עֶדְנָה
edna
pleasantness/menstruation

וַאדֹנִי   זָקֵן

v'adoni   *zaken*

and my master [masculine singular]   [is] old

11 Now Abraham and Sarah were old, and well stricken in age:
and it ceased to be with Sarah after the maner of women.
12 Therefore Sarah laughed within her selfe, saying, After I am
waxed old, shall I haue pleasure, my lord being old also?

> Genesis 18:11–12, King James Bible (1611)

11 Abraham and Sarah were old and getting on in years. Sarah
had passed the age of childbearing. 12 So she laughed to herself:
"After I have become shriveled up and my lord is old, will I have
delight?"

> Holman Christian Standard Bible (1999)

11 And Avraham and Sara were old, advanced in days,
the way of women had ceased for Sara.
12 Sara laughed within herself, saying:
After I have become worn, is there to be pleasure for
me? And my lord is old!

> Schocken Bible (*The Five Books of Moses*,
> translated by Everett Fox, 1997)

11 Now Abraham and Sarah were old, advanced in age; it had
ceased to be with Sarah after the manner of women. 12 So Sarah
laughed to herself, saying, "After I have grown old, and my husband is old, shall I have pleasure?"

> New Revised Standard Version,
> Catholic Edition (1989, 1993)

11 (Now Abraham and Sarah *were* old and stricken in age, *and* it
ceased to be with Sarah after the manner of women.)
12 Therefore Sarah laughed within herself, saying, After I am
waxed old, and my lord also, shall I have lust?
Footnote on verse 12: i. For she rather had respect to the order of nature,
than believed the promise of God.

Geneva Bible (1599)

11 Abraham and Sarah were already very old, and Sarah was
past the age of childbearing. 12 So Sarah laughed to herself as
she thought, "After I am worn out and my lord is old, will I now
have this pleasure?"

New International Version, 2011

———◆———

O NE OF MY BIGGEST FEARS IS THAT I WILL DIE BECAUSE I HAVE
talked too much. In my yeshiva day school, I was taught
that every human being has a limited number of words, and then
that's it—you're gone. Every few months I start worrying about
my tally, and I try to talk less. I warn my friends that a new, quieter
life lies ahead, but they don't believe me. Within days, my resolve
fades and I'm chattering again, letting the words pile up dangerously. Despite the fact that everyone in my family is familiar with
the threat of the constant ticking of words, most of my relatives
are cheerful, death-defying blabbermouths.

And yet, among the blabbermouths, there is my sister, who
utters a normal amount of words. Maybe that's why she gets so

much done. Once, in the middle of dinner, my parents complimented her on her magnificent, chatterless efficiency. She had, as usual, brought order to a huge array of bowls of soup to be salted and spiced, mounds of food to be taken out of ovens and placed on platters and matched with serving spoons—without talking about it. But she had an unusual reaction to the compliment. *"Emor me'at ve'aseh harbeh,"* she said. "Say little and do much." And then, very softly, she added: "It's the first thing you learn in school, from Avraham Avinu."

My sister was crediting Abraham, or, as she called him, Abraham our Father, for the way she goes about her work. The rest of us kept eating, stunned, for once, into silence. In the quiet, I thought again about how much our early life, how the way we read and heard the Bible, has affected all of my siblings. And so my sister, a management consultant and entrepreneur, sitting in front of me in perfectly ironed business clothes, cutting her food into pieces that were all exactly the same size—that sister noticed how Abraham rushed to get butter and milk, rushed to delegate, and coordinated all the tasks to welcome the visiting messengers who came to tell him he and Sarah would soon have a child. My sister noticed how swift he was, and how few words he needed to manage the entire experience. Slow and inefficient as I am, I never noticed how Abraham ran, how he did not make time to chat. In my universe of constant chatter, that grand, ancient, patriarchal quiet was impossible to hear.

I DID NOTICE SOMETHING ELSE about the story in Hebrew: how Sarah laughed. It is not a standard laugh. *Va'titzchak Sarah be'kirba.* Literally, it means "and Sarah laughed deep inside of herself." Or maybe more accurately: "And Sarah laughed in her gut." Many translations, like the 1989 New Revised Standard Version, Catholic Edition, try to make that neater, and so they say simply, "Sarah laughed to herself." But it's messier than that; it's an unusual laugh, and I wish that would come through more clearly in translation. Interestingly, some older translations like the King James and the Geneva Bible seem to emphasize the intense inner nature of this laugh more than newer translations do—they both choose "within herself" instead of the tamer "to herself."

How Sarah laughed reminds me of an earlier scene in the Garden of Eden, which was the last time in Genesis that what a woman heard and how she reacted to something a little difficult to process were at center stage. Some of the Bible's most resonant moments are depicted by gesture instead of speech. God sees; Eve eats the apple; Lot's wife turns back; and Sarah memorably laughs. "One thing is clear," my father says when the subject of Sarah comes up. "It was silent laughter, enabling Sarah later to deny that she laughed."

I am not certain that the laughter is clear. Perhaps understanding Sarah's laughter involves understanding the verses that frame it. Her laughter comes after several chapters of challenging circumstances—from relocation to a foreign place, where Abraham introduces her as his sister, to years of barrenness, to strife with her maid, who is also her husband's concubine. It comes after several verses that elaborately describe how old she is. They are verses full of speech, packed with detail.

All of this has not gone unnoticed by the biblical commentators who have scrutinized Sarah for thousands of years. In the rabbis' hands, the discussion of the intriguing triangle of Abraham, Sarah, and God becomes a conversation on how to behave.

* * *

Now, LOOKING BACK AT THE Bible, trying to understand how my sister and I could hear Abraham and Sarah so differently, I realize that the English doesn't emphasize Abraham's rushing about as much as the Hebrew does. In Hebrew, he's rushing in every sentence. In Genesis 18:6 and 18:7, the word "rush" appears twice and the word "run" appears once, all in a two-sentence span of Hebrew, whereas some English translations refer to running or rushing only twice. Here is a literal translation of those two verses, focusing on the meaning of the basic words and not the intricate grammatical issues that are present here as well:

> And Abraham rushed to the tent, to Sarah, and said, "Rush! Three measurements of the highest-quality flour. Knead it and make cakes."
> And Abraham ran to the cattle, and he took a young, good* calf and gave it to the servant, and the servant prepared it.

In the Yom Kippur prayers, there is a mention of how some people run with their legs to do evil. Abraham, of course, is the opposite: he runs and runs for good. After all this running, after Abraham extends his exemplary hospitality, the Bible does something very interesting. It starts repeating what we already know about Abraham and Sarah. This is especially strange because the passage has just showcased Abraham—as my sister pointed out— as doing a lot and not talking so much. Yet in the very same segment of text, the Bible feels the need to overtalk, to overtell, to say

---

* "Good" is a literal translation. It probably means a fat, healthy calf, which would be good to eat.

things a few times. It blabbers, like a person with no regard for a word count ticking away.

The blabbering starts with the basics—with the ages of Abraham and Sarah. We already know that Abraham is ninety-nine years old. But then in Genesis 18:11, the Bible tells us, in a very inefficient moment, that Abraham and Sarah are . . . old. It's true that ages in the Bible aren't the same as ages right now—Metushelach lived 969 years, after all—and maybe the Bible simply wants to emphasize their advanced ages.

But after telling us for the second time that Abraham and Sarah are old, the Bible adds, in literal Hebrew, that "a lot of days came" to Abraham and Sarah. The phrasing is an idiom, an ancient expression, that just means they are old. This is a classic example of what happens to biblical Hebrew idioms in translation. When faced with the oddness of a lot of days showing up, the English translations usually simplify and flatten: "days came" becomes the more reasonable-sounding "advanced in years." But while this translation is accurate, the literal Hebrew is lovely: a lot of days came. Just as one day after another turned my little sister into a young woman and a model of efficiency, so many days, coming one after another, made Sarah and Abraham old. The idea of days coming hints at the surprise of aging—in this case, the first description of old age in the Bible. Suddenly, one day after another: it happens. We focus on the day in front of us, the guest at the doorway, the meal to be made, and don't think that a lot of days, or a year, or a decade—or several decades—are now behind us. It's more reassuring to think of human life as days coming, and yet it's also a haunting way of explaining the quotidian nature of human aging, the inevitability of it.

But verse 11 does not stop there. After telling us that Abraham and Sarah are old, and that a lot of days came to them, in its

third attempt at describing what aging is, the Bible tells us that
Sarah no longer has *orach kanashim*. Literally, the phrase means
"the way of women." In Hebrew and in English, the Bible is coy.
Whereas the Jewish Publication Society translation spells it out—
"Sarah had stopped having the periods of women"—the English
is often translated as "the manner of women" or, in a literal translation, "the way of women." We readers are expected to know
what the way of women is, just as we are supposed to understand,
when the Bible says "and he knew his wife," that knowledge and
sex are synonyms. And this is yet another way of simply saying
that Sarah is old.

Here is Genesis 18:11, in the 1985 Jewish Publication Society
translation:

> Now Abraham and Sarah were old, advanced in years;
> Sarah had stopped having the periods of women.

Then the drama of the passage begins. Abraham presents the
messengers with a feast, and he stands nearby as they eat under a
tree. Meanwhile, Sarah is behind Abraham, in the tent, listening
at the door. I loved that detail as a child when I first read this, and
I still do. How like a writer Sarah is, always listening!

The great commentator Rashi understands Sarah's behavior
differently. He does not view it as eavesdropping, or as an expression of curiosity. Instead, Rashi explains that Sarah remained in
the tent when the angels came because she was modest. The word
Rashi uses to describe her—*tenuah*—is the same word used in one
of the most haunting of the Torah's commands: *Walk modestly
before Adonai your God*. The Talmud, which is both a legal text
and an extensive discussion of the law and the Bible, discusses

Sarah's presence in the tent, too, and it focuses on why the messengers asked where Sarah was. Surely the angels knew she was in the tent. Finally, Rav Yehuda concludes that the angels posed the question in order to endear Sarah to her husband, to remind him of her modesty.

From her hidden perch, Sarah hears the angel say she'll have a child within a year. In the English, the Oxford Annotated Bible primly says: "Sarah laughed to herself, saying, 'After I have grown old, and my husband is old, shall I have pleasure?'"

THE RABBIS ARE EXTREMELY INTERESTED in two questions the verse raises: How, exactly, did Sarah laugh, and why did she laugh at all? Both of these questions are motivated by individual words in Hebrew that are more challenging than they appear in translation. The two problematic words are the Hebrew *be'kirba*, often translated as "to herself," and the word *edna*, which is translated here as "pleasure."

The commentators tackle this situation word by word. Rashi reads in the word *edna*, meaning "pleasure" or "delight," the word *idan*—or "time," which he interprets as a period of blood. Interestingly, the modern Hebrew dictionary Even-Shoshan translates *edna* itself as "menstruation." What Abraham cannot give Sarah is not pleasure here but time—that is, her time, her menstrual blood. Abraham can't give her the years back. When Sarah laughs, the reader understands that it is humorous to imagine that Abraham, a mere man, can turn back time. Ibn Janach, the eleventh-century grammarian and lexicographer, defines the three-letter root in *edna* as *ayin, daled, nun*. That root, he says, conveys pleasantness and delight. He offers several examples of how the root appears in the Bible. When he arrives at the Sarah episode, he sees *edna* as "youth." The ninety-nine-year-old Abraham can't give Sarah youth.

But there are alternatives to this word-by-word approach. Interestingly, the Midrash understands the verse of Sarah laughing not as a question but as a statement. Since there is no punctuation in the Hebrew Torah scroll, it's always a matter of discussion. On this verse the Talmud quotes Rav Hisda, who says that on that day, Sarah returned to the physical appearance of her youth—the wrinkles left, and her period came back. In other words, she may have been old, but she looked pleasing and became nubile.

All of this discussion of why Sarah laughed in verse 12 is heightened by verse 13. The rabbis of the Talmud are extremely interested in why Sarah says, in Genesis 18:12, that *Abraham* is old, and then three verses later, God reports on the episode, describing Sarah as asking whether she can have a child, because *she* is old, with no mention of Abraham's age.

The Bible clearly records this discrepancy: in the translation and in the original, God does not report the situation exactly as it occurred. God says to Abraham, in the Oxford Annotated version, "Why did Sarah laugh, and say, 'Shall I indeed bear a child, now that I am old? Is anything too wonderful for the Lord?'"

Yet Sarah's expressed doubt is not just about her own age but about Abraham's, and it gets the rabbis going. They wonder if Sarah found Abraham rather withered and—well, a little disappointing. In God's version, how old Abraham is—and if the rabbis of the Talmud are right to imply this, how capable a lover Sarah thought Abraham was, or could be, at ninety-nine—is no longer part of the conversation. The rabbis discuss this further, to my delight, saying that God edited Sarah's version of the story deliberately. In the New King James Version, the section reads:

12 Therefore Sarah laughed within herself, saying, "After
I have grown old, shall I have pleasure, my lord being old
also?"
13 And the Lord said to Abraham, "Why did Sarah laugh,
saying, 'Shall I surely bear a child, since I am old?'"

The Talmud's discussion seems to indicate that God knew
Sarah laughed because she found Abraham a little disappointing.
What matters to God, the Talmud suggests, is that Abraham and
Sarah get along. And so God doesn't share what some readers
interpret as Sarah's editorializing on Abraham's sexual abilities,
or perhaps Sarah's general feeling that Abraham is too old to be
a father. God's peaceful solution is to take the blame on himself,
asking Abraham, Does she not think that I, God, can create a
son? "Great is peace," says Rabbi Ishmael, "for even the Holy
One blessed be He, deviated [from the truth] on account of it."
Maybe God is taking a cue from Abraham, too. He, too, says little
and does much. He rushes to take action, making Abraham think
Sarah doubted God. He reports the entire episode to Abraham in
one brief line. I love the way everyone has their own scheme, their
own way of reading reality, even God.

And now the rabbis' second question seems relevant. How
did Sarah laugh? What does "laughing inside" mean?

Onkelos, whose first-century commentary is a translation of
the Hebrew into Aramaic, has Sarah smiling, not laughing. And
then he has her smiling in one of her intestines! It's bizarre, kind
of crazy, that word *beeme'ah'hah*, which Onkelos uses to define
Sarah's laugh, but he's trying to capture the oddness of the laugh
in Hebrew—the interiority of it.

I'm so entertained when I discover that Sarah's laugh—or her
smile, if Onkelos is right—happens in only one of her intestines

that I call my mother to discuss it. She explains that in both Hebrew and English, descriptions of bodily position often involves prepositions, but in Hebrew, as one of her professors explained to her, most prepositions actually are body parts. "Next to" is rendered, literally, as *al yad*—"on the hand of." To indicate that something is "on top of," "over," or "above," Hebrew generally uses *al p'nei*—literally, "on the face of." This preposition appears in Genesis 1:2, with the wind of God moving along, literally, "the face of the water," which some translations render simply as "over the water." Here, Sarah's intestine, when used as a preposition, actually means inside, or within. "Most commentators don't go to the trouble of telling you she laughed in her intestine," my mother says. "They'll say she laughs inside her, or in her heart."

However Sarah laughed, however she defined delight, and whatever she really thought of Abraham, I imagine her as one of those people who know how to let their entire body be taken over with laughter. Everything she had learned in the world was in that laugh. I'm rooting for Sarah, hoping her gutsiness comes through in English translation, but it doesn't always. "Sarah laughed to herself" is what I usually find, and that gives the reader no clue that there might be a little more going on. I am moved by her laughter, and not only because it comes from an old woman, one the Talmud sees as brave enough to possibly allude to her husband's bedroom technique while God's angels were in the vicinity. I am moved because it is the first laugh in the whole Bible. Here, after eighteen chapters, someone finally laughs.

That laughter does not go unnoticed. God flat-out asks Sarah why she has laughed—but Sarah denies it. Many of the commentators chatter about why Sarah denies laughing, and most say simply—because she was afraid.

Ha! I've never thought of Sarah as afraid. Sarah brazenly does what God does in this episode: she edits the truth. If, according to Rabbi Ishmael, God decided that leaving a few details out would help keep a married couple together, Sarah seems to think along the same editorial and psychological lines. But when Sarah denies her laughter, she's not trying to hold on to her man. Instead, she seems to change her story to preserve a different relationship— the relationship between herself and God. In Sarah's effort to hold on to her portion of divine love, she pushes her laughter so deep inside herself that when she tells God her version of the story, her laughter doesn't exist at all.

Still, Sarah and her laughter have a power over us. For centuries, her laugh has been examined, debated, questioned. It is, after all, a direct challenge to God—an outright laugh at divine plans for humans. And even if we finally say we understand exactly why Sarah laughed, there is still one big problem with this intriguing episode: whether Abraham ever knows why Sarah truly laughed is not disclosed. Did Abraham wonder about it? Did he know the reason in his heart? The Bible simply does not tell us. And maybe this private, silent aspect of Abraham is what makes him so cinematic. Because we are not let in on what Abraham thinks, we are left to wonder what was going on in his mind, here as in the binding of Isaac—his son whose name means "will laugh," after Sarah's laughter. After all these centuries, Abraham remains a lone man on the stage, singular and determined and seemingly full of faith in an unseen God.

MAN

בֵּיהּ וְנָסִיבַת מֵאִבֵּהּ
וַאֲכָלַת וִיהָבַת אַף לְבַעְלַהּ
עִמַּהּ וַאֲכָל: ז וְאִתְפַּתַּחָא
עֵינֵי תַרְוֵיהוֹן וִידָעוּ אֲרֵי
עַרְטִלָּאִין אִנּוּן וְחַטִּיטוּ
לְהוֹן טַרְפֵי תֵאֵנִין וַעֲבָדוּ
לְהוֹן זָרְזִין: ח וּשְׁמָעוּ יַת
קָל מֵימְרָא דַיָי אֱלֹהִים
דִּמְהַלֵּךְ בְּגִנְתָא לִמְנַח
יוֹמָא וְאִטְּמַר אָדָם
וְאִתְּתֵיהּ מִן קֳדָם יְיָ
אֱלֹהִים בְּגוֹ אִילָן גִּנְתָא:
ט וּקְרָא יְיָ אֱלֹהִים לְאָדָם
וַאֲמַר לֵיהּ אָן אַתְּ:

לְהַשְׂכִּיל וַתִּקַּח מִפִּרְיוֹ וַתֹּאכַל וַתִּתֵּן
גַּם־לְאִישָׁהּ עִמָּהּ וַיֹּאכַל: ז וַתִּפָּקַחְנָה
עֵינֵי שְׁנֵיהֶם וַיֵּדְעוּ כִּי עֵירֻמִּם הֵם
וַיִּתְפְּרוּ עֲלֵה תְאֵנָה וַיַּעֲשׂוּ לָהֶם
חֲגֹרֹת: ח וַיִּשְׁמְעוּ אֶת־קוֹל יְהוָה
אֱלֹהִים מִתְהַלֵּךְ בַּגָּן לְרוּחַ הַיּוֹם
וַיִּתְחַבֵּא הָאָדָם וְאִשְׁתּוֹ מִפְּנֵי יְהוָה
אֱלֹהִים בְּתוֹךְ עֵץ הַגָּן: ט וַיִּקְרָא
יְהוָה אֱלֹהִים אֶל־הָאָדָם וַיֹּאמֶר לוֹ

תו"א ... ז ויתפרו עלה. ברכות נ"ו סנהדרין ע"א ...
ויקרא ... נ' סנהדרין ל"ח

רש"י

וַתִּתֵּן גַּם לְאִישָׁהּ. שֶׁלֹּא תָמוּת הִיא וִיחְיֶה הוּא וְיִשָּׂא
אַחֶרֶת. גַּם. לְרַבּוֹת בְּהֵמָה וְחַיָּה: (ז) וַתִּפָּקַחְנָה וְגו'.
לְעִנְיַן הַחָכְמָה דִּבֵּר הַכָּתוּב וְלֹא לְעִנְיַן רְאִיָּה מַמָּשׁ וְסוֹף
הַמִּקְרָא מוֹכִיחַ: וַיֵּדְעוּ כִּי עֵירֻמִּים הֵם. אַף הַסּוּמָא יוֹדֵעַ
כְּשֶׁהוּא עָרוֹם אֶלָּא מַהוּ וַיֵּדְעוּ כִּי עֵירֻמִּים הֵם...

שפתי חכמים

...

אבן עזרא

שֶׁלֹּא יִתֵּן גַּם לְאִשָּׁה יוֹסֵי לְחַיֵּי הָאָדָם קל"ב: (ח) וַיִּשְׁמְעוּ מִתְהַלֵּךְ
בַּגָּן. קוֹל הַשֵּׁם וְזֶה הָיָה...

אור החיים

הַבְּתֵי הֵיכָרַת בְּלֹא טְעִימָה וַחֲלוּקָה זוֹ אֵל הַהַשְׂכָּלָה אֵינָהּ...

רמב"ן

וְהַכְּלָל כִּי בּוֹ יִרְצֶה וְיַחְפֹּץ בְּדָבָר אוֹ בִּהְפֹּכוֹ: (ז) וַתְּפַקַּחְנָה...

כלי יקר

וַתִּתֵּן לְאִישָׁהּ עִמָּהּ...

וַיִּשְׁמְעוּ
Vayishmeh'oo
And they heard

אֶת־
et
[no English equivalent
introduces a definite
direct object]

קוֹל
kol
[the] voice/
sound

יְהוָה
adonai
God
[Literally, *adonai* = "my masters" (plural)]

אֱלֹהִים
elohim
God

מִתְהַלֵּךְ
mithalech
walking

בַּגָּן
bagan
in the garden

לָרוּחַ
l'ruach
in the wind
[literally, "to
the wind"]

הַיּוֹם
hayom
of the day

וַיִּתְחַבֵּא
Vayitchabeh
And he hid

הָאָדָם
ha'adam
the man

וְאִשְׁתּוֹ
v'ishto
and his wife

מִפְּנֵי
mip'nei
from the face of

יְהוָה
adonai
God

אֱלֹהִים
elohim
God

בְּתוֹךְ
betoch
inside

עֵץ
etz
tree [collective
noun]

הַגָּן
hagan
the garden

8 And they heard the voyce of the LORD God, walking in the garden in the coole of the day: and Adam and his wife hid themselues from the presence of the LORD God, amongst the trees of the garden.

9 And the LORD God called vnto Adam, and said vnto him, Where art thou?

Genesis 3:8–9, King James Bible (1611)

8 And there came to them the sound of the Lord God walking in the garden in the evening wind: and the man and his wife went to a secret place among the trees of the garden, away from the eyes of the Lord God.

9 And the voice of the Lord God came to the man, saying, Where are you?

Darby Bible (1890)

8 And they heard the voice of the LORD God walking in the garden toward the cool of the day; and the man and his wife hid themselves from the presence of the LORD God amongst the trees of the garden.

9 And the LORD God called unto the man, and said unto him: "Where art thou?"

Jewish Publication Society Bible (1917)

8 And they hear the sound of Jehovah God walking up and down in the garden at the breeze of the day, and the man and his wife hide themselves from the face of Jehovah God in the midst of the trees of the garden.

9 And Jehovah God calleth unto the man, and saith to him, "Where [art] thou?"

Robert Young, *Young's Literal Translation* (1898)

8 And they heard the voice of the Lord God going in the garden
to the direction of the sun, and the man and his wife hid from
before the Lord God in the midst of the trees of the garden.
9 And the Lord God called to man, and He said to him, "Where
are you?"

Judaica Press Bible (translated by Rabbi A. J. Rosenberg, 2005)

8 Now they heard the sound of YHWH, God, [who was] walk-
ing about in the garden at the breezy-time of the day.
And the human and his wife hid themselves from the face of
YHVH, God, amid the trees of the garden.
9 YHWH, God, called to the human and said to him:
Where are you?

Schocken Bible (*The Five Books of Moses*,
translated by Everett Fox, 1997)

———◆———

J UST AS ISAAC BEGINS IN LAUGHTER AND IS NAMED FOR IT, SO MAN
in the Bible begins with his name. The first man we meet is
Adam, who is named for *adama*, or earth. In fact, in Hebrew, *adam*
is the word for "man." But Adam the man—that first human on
the stage of the world—is bizarrely earthless in English, and so is
mankind. The essential connection between man and the earth
is missing. Without the reader's knowing at all times that Adam
is *adama*—the ground he walks on, labors in, and will eventually
return to—and without the reader's understanding that Adam is
also everyman, Adam's name doesn't mark him in the same intense, intimate, and obvious way in translation.

Eve, too, has a symbolic name; Chava, as Eve is named in Hebrew, comes from the word *chayim*, which means "life" in Hebrew. We know this because Adam, who names Eve in Genesis 3:20, explains that Chava is *em kol chai*—the mother of all life. For an English speaker, the link between *chai* and *Chava* may seem weak. But in Hebrew, as Ibn Ezra explains, the letter *yud*, or the English *y*, and the letter *vav*, or what is rendered as a *v* in English, can be flipped. This switch occurs elsewhere in the Bible. Ibn Ezra explains further that *em kol chai* refers to humans, not all living things, and that it is important to separate the name Chava from *chaya*, which means animal. Ibn Janach, the eleventh-century grammarian and lexicographer, agrees with Ibn Ezra. He lists the root for Chava's name as *chet, yud, hey*, and also explains that the letters *vav* and *yud* are flipped in Hebrew.

But despite these medieval commentators' efforts to explain how Chava and *chayim* are linked, it is difficult if not impossible to hear the link between "Eve" and "life" in translation. In the King James Version, for instance, the verse reads: "And Adam called his wife's name Eve; because she was the mother of all living." The logic here must befuddle the reader of English.

All the biblical real estate devoted to who was named what and why, along with when and where, can seem odd and tedious, even pointless, to an English reader. But to a Hebrew reader, the Bible's names are a big part of its meaning. From Adam onward, at nearly every turn in the Bible, the names of men, women, and children have clear meanings, and they often represent physical reality and emotional destiny. Yet the meanings of these Hebrew names are lost in translation because the names are usually simply transliterated—not translated (although Eve's name is neither; it has no relation in sound or meaning to the Hebrew).

Consider the patriarchs. Their names often reflect one of two essential moments in their lives—the circumstances of their birth, as in the case of Isaac, who is named for his mother's laughter, or their encounter with God. These episodes tend to be fairly dramatic; sometimes, patriarchs' names reflect both these episodes, as in the case of Jacob, who is later renamed Israel. Ya'akov, as Jacob is known in Hebrew, received that name because he held on to the *akev*, or heel, of his brother as he made his way through the birth canal. The younger boy's name says it all: *ya'akov* in modern Hebrew means "he will follow."

When Jacob's name is changed after he encounters the angel, Ya'akov, or Jacob, becomes Yisrael, or Israel. The name Yisrael is a combination of a verb that means "to rule" in the future tense—*yisrah*—and *el*, a noun that means "God." Traditionally, the episode is translated as "Jacob fought with the angel" or "warred with him." But Jacob didn't just fight with the angel, as many translations insist; he *overcame* the angel, and so ruled over a creature more powerful than he. This is critical; in fact, this small linguistic point may be why Israel's first prime minister, David Ben-Gurion, chose Jacob's new name, Israel, for the new state; he hoped the new country, like the patriarch Jacob, would overcome impossible odds, not simply fight.

THE BIBLE ITSELF INSISTS THAT names matter. The prophet Isaiah promises the Jewish people *yad vashem*, literally, a hand and a name, and figuratively, a monument and a name. The translator of Isaiah in the 1972 Jewish Publication Society edition was the towering scholar H. L. Ginsberg, who renders Isaiah 56:5 this way:

> I will give them, in My House
> And within My walls,

A monument and a name
Better than sons or daughters.
I will give them **an everlasting name**
Which shall not perish.

Isaiah understood that names and survival are intertwined. Today, the Holocaust museum in Israel is named Yad VaShem after this verse in Isaiah: the museum aims to outlast death by naming it, especially after so many of the dead were last identified by a tattooed number—not a name. Names are considered so important in Jewish tradition that according to rabbinic commentary (Vayikra Rabbah 32:5), clinging to their names was one of the four reasons the ancient Israelites were freed from their slavery. But the idea of using a name to define life is as old as Adam and Eve. In the beginning, as Genesis 1:26 relates, God creates man in his image, and man is referred to by God as *ha'adam*. In verse 27, man and woman are simply male and female. Then man is given the power to name all the animals, which he does. Only in Genesis 3:20 is Eve, whose name contains life itself, named by Adam, her husband. But the first human name given in the Bible—Adam—is selected by God.

BEING NAMED BY GOD DOES not help Adam. "Cursed is the ground because of you," the translation insists in Genesis 3:17, in the 2001 English Standard Version translation from Crossway Bibles, trying to capture the famous and unforgettable curse uttered to Adam. What is so terrible about the curse and the sweat that Adam, the first man, is condemned to when he leaves the garden is that Adam himself comes from earth, is named for it, and returns to it, and yet that same earth—his namesake—will not respond to his hands.

The exact location of the earth-man Adam's sweat differs in various translations. In the solid Oxford translation of Genesis 3:19, it is "by the sweat of your face you shall eat bread until you return to the ground," and in the 1985 Jewish Publication Society translation, it is "by the sweat of your brow shall you get bread to eat."

I remember the way the Hebrew words looked to me as a seven-year-old. *Ze'at apeicha.* The sweat of your nose. *Apeicha* literally means "of your nose," from the word *af,* which means "nose." As a child reading about Adam's punishment, I would wonder how many hours of labor it would take before the nose would start to dissolve into beads of sweat. How much harder it is for the nose to drip sweat than just the cheeks, or the place where hair meets skin. Adam's punishment is to work hard, to struggle with an unresponsive earth, all the days of his life, until he dies—in other words, he has to work himself to death. And he would feel the difficulty of his labor in his nose—space of breath, connection between the human and the air, between man and the clouds.

OTHER INTERESTING THINGS HAPPEN TO Adam in translation. In Genesis 3:8, according to the 2001 New Oxford Annotated Bible, Adam and Eve "heard the sound of the Lord God walking in the garden at the time of the evening breeze, and the man and his wife hid themselves from the presence of the Lord God among the trees of the garden."

Wait. Is God actually *walking*?

When I began reading English translations, I promised myself to read English on its own terms: to read deeply before looking back at the Hebrew. But this sudden insertion of the body— the hint of divine feet—is just too much. I can't help myself. I walk out to the car where my Hebrew Bibles are locked and peek at the Hebrew of Genesis 3:8 in the light from the open car door. It is just what I suspected; there in the garden is just what I remember: the voice of God. The Hebrew reads:

Vayishmeh'oo et kol adonai elohim mithalech bagan.

At least I had always understood the word *kol* as the voice of God moving through the garden. But then I stop and consider: *kol* means "voice," but it also means "sound." In this verse, as in so many others, meaning is a question of context. The problem here is not just the translation of one word, *kol*, but how to translate it in combination with *mithalech*, a form of the verb "to walk" that refers to a specific manner of walking. The question is what or who is "walking" in this specific way—a being or a voice? Is it a creature taking a walk through the garden, or is it a voice making its way through the lush vegetation?

IN ANY CASE, THE SOUND of God walking seems to imply that God has a body. I think of Adam's curse, the way it becomes the sweat of his face and not just a part of the face in some translations. It seems that often whatever is bodily is blurred, transformed in translators' hands. The body, it seems, is a battleground in translation. The ancient Bible often relies on body parts in its metaphors and descriptions, which is not necessarily a contemporary way of viewing the world. Translated literally, these metaphors can seem awkward, bizarre, or overly dramatic in English. And yet in dropping these body parts from their translations, the translators may be losing an important component of the ancient world's understanding of the body: the physical as a reference point for the world around it.

There are no feet in Genesis 3:8, just an intriguing verb: *mithalech*. This particular grammatical construction of the three-letter root for the verb "to walk" is used for doing something repeatedly. If *holech*, or walk, in the present tense, means to walk from point A to point B, then *mithalech* means to walk from point A to B to D to C—walking back and forth, walking repeatedly, or without a particular destination in mind.

Is it possible that God himself is wandering? Could God himself actually be walking?

I walk through Iowa City thinking about whether God really walks. I pass the old houses, the brown one with the little window porch that I love, and the pink one I didn't buy because the agent said it had termites. I wonder if what is said is ever the truth: the reading and rereading has made me wonder about whatever I first hear and first believe. Perhaps there are termites inside, or perhaps the agent, who then warmly led me to a tiny blue house that has brought me great joy, is only repeating what she heard.

I decide to call my favorite grammarian. I ask my mother what she thinks of this God walking stuff. Maybe the translation in which God is on a walk is right, I say cautiously.

"What we have here is unusual syntax," my mother says. We look again at the Hebrew.

"What *mithalech* means," my mother explains, "is that you can hear the voice of God from all directions in the garden. God asks Adam where he is, and so the voice is going in different directions, repeatedly. Grammatically, *mithalech* means that something must be repeating."

It's the voice, my mother insists, not the feet, that is taking a walk.

I wonder what other people, in past centuries, have thought—whether it is God walking, or his voice. My mother and I look at Rashi. The great medieval commentator does something odd here: he tells us what *not* to think, what answer not to arrive at. Rashi wants to make sure we don't think the passage is referring to God walking.

Rashi anticipates the King James and other recent translations, and warns against this image of God on a stroll. "Well," my mother says, "it's a complicated passage. I can see how they get it, but I don't think so."

I GO BACK TO THE King James. "Cursed is the ground for thy sake," Genesis 3:17 reads. Here "cursed" serves as an adjective, just as it does in Hebrew. I am moved by the idea that the ground is cursed because of Adam's behavior. And of course, the ground's curse makes Adam's life far more difficult. With the labor he is now condemned to, he is cursed by what he is, by his namesake, by the earth he is made of.

I understand this feeling of being chased from the inside. Even in Iowa, I am still ruled by language and memory, grammar and God. I can't even walk down the street without thinking of Adam's nose or face or God's body or voice.

When I speak to my mother again, she tells me that my childhood reading of *af* as "nose" is incorrect, that in the language of the Bible, an ancient Hebrew no longer spoken, *af* means "face." In Semitic languages, she explains, at times a part represents the whole. So the nose, as the most obvious section of the face, refers to the face. This was explained to her by the late professor Moshe Held, she tells me. That must be why some translations translate

Adam's brow or nose as his face. How embarrassing, to realize how much I read incorrectly.

Yet the wrong reading is often more exciting than the right one. I like the idea of nose better than face. I like the awfulness of nose-sweat; it feels like a curse. Maybe there is something in us that loves our own mistakes, something human.

ENCOURAGED BY THE IDEA THAT the body matters, I spend more time thinking about God's nose than my electric bill, the various financial scandals plaguing the country, and the state of our democracy. My friend the minister's son encourages me to keep going, tells me that in all his reading of the Bible he never experienced anything about the body of Adam coming through the translation. He never thought much about where, exactly, Adam's sweat comes from.

I scour dictionaries and surround myself with notes of biblical references to the nose and other body parts. The Hebrew dictionary Even-Shoshan, considered the authoritative modern dictionary of the Hebrew language, looks at the nose and anger together and calls it a big anger, a frothing anger. Even-Shoshan functions like the Oxford English Dictionary, offering examples of the way in which a word is used, and because it is discussing Hebrew, the examples are often from the Bible. Here, as an example, Even-Shoshan quotes Isaiah 13:13. "Therefore shall heaven be shaken, / And earth leap out of its place / At the fury of the Lord of Hosts / on the day of His burning wrath." So translates H. L. Ginsberg, my favorite Isaiah translator. That "burning wrath" is *charon af* in Hebrew, anger of the nose, or more specifically, here it is in possessive form, *charon apo*. Ginsberg writes: his burning wrath. His nose wrath, I want to say, so that English readers get a glimpse of the body part inside the ancient metaphor.

By editing out the *af*, Ginsberg edits out the froth, too: the widening of the nostrils, the huffing of the air.

My father, who is as interested as I am in biblical omission, calls much too early in the morning to discuss this question of the nose. Forty years ago, he tells me, he had a Hebrew teacher who said that when a person gets angry, his nostrils expand. They flare. He is referring to what I have already sensed: that the translations that edit out the *af* also edit out the froth.

My father also wants to discuss the word *charon*, whose root means "to burn." Like me, my mathematician father likes to break a problem into parts. "Don't forget," he tells me, "we're talking burning anger here."

The ancient metaphor *charon apo* is often translated simply as "his wrath." Perhaps it is more accurately translated as "burning anger," as my father suggests, or "burning wrath," as Ginsberg renders it. All of those meanings—the burning like a fire, the widening of the nose—are part of the phrase. And maybe wrath is like that; it is bodily and fiery and expansive.

IN MY FAMILY, ANYTHING BIBLICAL easily expands into a long discussion. I know that in a few hours, my mother will call to disagree with my father's nose comments, and with mine.

Just as I predicted, the phone rings. "There's something else that's fascinating here," my mother says. "The opposite of *charon af*—literally, burning of the nose—is *erech appayim*, which literally would be the length of the noses, plural, and figuratively means patience or a conquest of anger, a restraint." My mother is referring to Exodus 34:6, where the phrase *erech appayim* appears. It is the passage in which God asks Moses to cut two tablets of stone, and then God descends from the clouds and proclaims:

> The Lord, the Lord, a God merciful and gracious, slow
> to anger, and abounding in steadfast love and faithfulness,
> keeping steadfast love for the thousandth generation, for-
> giving iniquity and transgression and sin.

The plural of *af* is *appayim*. The word *appayim* appears not only in this passage, but in the thirteen properties of God mentioned over and over in the Yom Kippur liturgy, which quotes this passage. In Hebrew, it is intoned as practically a mantra: *"Adonai, adonai, el rachum v'chanun, erech appayim v'rav chesed v'emet."*

That "slow to anger" phrase, so famous in all the depictions of a patient, merciful God, is actually *erech appayim*—long of face, or to be super-literal, perhaps long of noses. Figuratively, it describes a slowly angering God, a God whose patience is depicted through his body, a God whose nostrils take a while to flare out. It's an expression, a metaphor, not a collection of words read individually, but maybe it should be for a moment; maybe the nose in the phrase matters.

But even if *appayim* does not mean "noses" and actually means "faces," following the principle that in ancient languages a part is a metaphor for the whole, that's still weird. That means that God is described, literally at least, as having two faces. Still, I am intrigued by the idea of two faces as an expression of patience— especially as opposed to contemporary English, in which "two-faced" connotes deception.

"So what's going on here? It's not clear," my mother says.

I sigh. More biblical ambiguity that I will just have to live with.

"A person gets angry and his nostrils get red," my mother

continues, focusing on what she can explain. "It's like *katzaf.*" *Katzaf* is the Hebrew word for "froth." But in translation, *vayiktzof*—literally, "and he frothed"—becomes simply "he got angry," just as God's nose-expanding wrath becomes simply God's anger or God's wrath.

"A person froths at the mouth, and burns at the nose," my mother says.

So far, so good. That much makes sense. Then I make the mistake of bringing up the plural again. "The plural is a problem, and the whole idea of face is a problem," my mother says. "But this is what's so interesting."

So these intriguing ancient expressions don't always make complete sense—at least to a contemporary reader. Maybe it's unfair to ask a translator to translate ambiguity, to preserve what is difficult enough to comprehend in Hebrew and make it similarly baffling in English. In any case, in translation, both nose burning and mouth frothing are often described as simple anger, not as bodily anger. The reader of English often has no idea that the body was even part of the phrase.

Throughout the Bible, the body is often the signpost of emotion—for God and man. Pharaoh "hardens his heart" to avoid letting his slaves, the people of Israel, go free. The people of Israel, when taken out of Egypt, are described as "stiff-necked," which means stubborn.

And as I've already mentioned, the body also often acts as an indicator of physical placement. In both Hebrew and English, bodily position often involves prepositions, but in Hebrew, most prepositions actually are body parts. The body matters not only because it can indicate what is going on and precisely where, but also because it sometimes functions figuratively as a signpost of morality. Adam sweating out his destiny on his brow in order to earn the bread he puts in his mouth because he betrayed God's instructions is very different from Adam simply sweating. The body in the Bible is specific, and the degree of bodily detail makes the narrative more intimate, more personal, more deeply human.

NOSE, BROW, FACE — IT'S ONLY THE beginning. I continue on my project of reading the Bible in translation, looking for moments where the body is blurred or erased. Exhausted by Genesis, I try Exodus.

It doesn't take long to find an example. Exodus begins with a list of descendants who come out of *yerech Ya'akov*—the thigh of Jacob. Some commentators say that "thigh" is a figure of speech for the penis. The King James Version is surprisingly racy, calling it his loins. But other translations omit thigh, penis, and loins entirely and just say, rather chastely, that Jacob's descendants went down to Egypt. Their readers never get to visualize the image of a whole people coming from a thigh, of slavery originating in one body part.

As I keep reading and accumulating translations, I notice that some translations do mention the body imagery in the notes. In Exodus 6:30, Moses describes himself with the Hebrew phrase *arel s'fataim*, which the 2001 New Oxford Annotated Bible translates as "a poor speaker."

In the Oxford, the entire verse reads:

But Moses said in the LORD's presence, "since I **am a poor speaker**, why would Pharaoh listen to me?"

I sigh with disappointment at this word choice. But then I see the note explaining that in Hebrew *arel s'fataim* means "uncircumcised of lips." More than simply conveying "I don't speak very well," the ancient metaphor tries to say, "I am not ready, I am not worthy, I have not been okayed for the task." It also means "I'm not that good at speaking." So while the Oxford's translation of the verse is technically correct, the omission of the bodily uncircumcised lips takes the nuance out of the meaning, and it also distances us from how the ancients expressed themselves. The Hebrew words give the reader a glimpse into the personality of Moses, into the character of a man who felt his lips were not fit for the task of leadership.

I CALL HOME AGAIN.

"There's so much that isn't translated about the body," I say to my brother Davi, who happens to be home to pick up the receiver. Davi's apartment in Manhattan is only a forty-minute bus ride away, so I'm not surprised that he's there visiting.

Davi points out that the Bible contradicts itself on the body— Moses tells the people of Israel that they have seen God face-to-face, but in another passage, God insists that no one can see God and live. Davi quotes Deuteronomy 5:4—"The Lord spoke with you **face to face** at the mountain, out of the fire," in the 2001 New Oxford Annotated Bible translation. That directly conflicts with Exodus 33:18–23, which Davi quickly quotes for me in Hebrew from memory. Davi is a *ba'al koreh*, someone who reads the Torah out loud in synagogue, and he has therefore chanted the Torah in its entirety many times, and has memorized large swaths of it.

I remember that section, and so I hang up the phone and go back to my piles of Bibles in translation. The drama of Exodus 33:18–23 begins with Moses begging for a glimpse of God. In the Crossway Bible (2011), the passage reads:

Moses said, "Please show me your glory." And he said, "I will make all my goodness pass before you and will proclaim before you my name 'The LORD.' And I will be gracious to whom I will be gracious, and will show mercy on whom I will show mercy. But," he said, "**you cannot see my face, for man shall not see me and live.**" And the LORD said, "Behold, there is a place by me where you shall stand on the rock, and while my glory passes by I will put you in a cleft of the rock, and I will cover you with my hand until I have passed by. Then I will take away my hand, and you shall see my back, but my face shall not be seen."

My brother Davi is right: the two sections—one in Exodus and one in Deuteronomy—do not reconcile. But the Exodus text actually contradicts itself, too. In one part of the text, God explicitly says that no human can see God and live. In another part, God allows Moses to see the divine back. What does this contradiction mean? Was the divine back a metaphor—some ancient expression we no longer understand?

And perhaps these questions are the reasons why the body is erased or minimized in translation. A modern-day editor would have insisted that Exodus and Deuteronomy take the same stance on the body of God. But the Bible was originally intended for ancient ears. And so the language of the body is employed for the most essential situations: blessing, promise, curse, vocation. Blessings are often given through hands on the head; a promise is a hand on a thigh, as when Eliezer promises Abraham he will find a bride for Isaac; a curse can be seen on a face, as we have seen with Adam and also with Cain; and when the angel of God burns Isaiah's lips, the reader can hear undeniable vocation. All of these are descriptive, but they all involve destiny. For my modern ears, the most haunting use of the body and its metaphors is the rather sinister destiny that is in play when human freedom is at stake—which is what happens with slavery.

וַיָּשִׂימוּ	עָלָיו	שָׂרֵי	מִסִּים
Vayasimoo	*alav*	*sarei*	*misim*
And they put	upon them	masters/ministers	taxes; forced labor

[Literally, *alav* means "upon him," but it's a collective pronoun.]

לְמַעַן	עַנֹּתוֹ		בְּסִבְלֹתָם
l'ma'an	*anohto*		*b'sivlotam*
in order to	torture him		with their suffering
	[a collective noun here]		

וַיִּבֶן	עָרֵי	מִסְכְּנוֹת	לְפַרְעֹה
vayeeven	*arei*	*miskenot*	*l'Pharaoh*
and he built	cities	storage/treasure	for Pharaoh

[Even-Shoshan's Hebrew dictionary says *miskenot* comes from the Akkadian *maškanu*, or "to store."]

אֶת־		פִּתֹם
et		*Pitom*
[no English equivalent; introduces definite direct object]		Pitom [name of city]

וְאֶת־		רַעַמְסֵס
ve'et		*Ra'amses*
and *et*		Ra'amses [name of city]

וְכַאֲשֶׁר
v'cha'asher
and as; and
the more

יְעַנּוּ
yeh'ahnoo
they tortured

אֹתוֹ
oto
him [here a collective direct
object pronoun meaning "them"]

כֵּן
ken
so

יִרְבֶּה
yirbeh
he got
more
numerous

וְכֵן
v'chen
and so

יִפְרֹץ
yiphrotz
he stretched out;
expanded; took
up more space

["He" here is a collective pronoun meaning "they."]

וַיָּקֻצוּ
va'yakootzoo
and they got
disgusted

מִפְּנֵי
mip'nei
with [literally,
"from the
face of"]

בְּנֵי
b'nei
children

יִשְׂרָאֵל
yisrael
Israel
[phrase = "children of Israel"]

וַיַּעֲבִדוּ
Va'yaaveedoo
And they made [them] work;
and they enslaved [them]

מִצְרַיִם
mitzrayim
Egypt/Egyptians

אֶת־
et
[see *et* above]

בְּנֵי
b'nei
children/sons

יִשְׂרָאֵל
yisrael
[of] Israel [another name for
Jacob; entire phrase is
"children of Israel"]

בְּפָרֶךְ
b'pharech
in breaking [meaning "in body-breaking labor"]

11 Therefore they did set ouer them task-masters, to afflict them with their burdens: And they built for Pharaoh treasure-cities, Pithom and Raamses.

12 But the more they afflicted them, the more they multiplied and grew: and they were grieued because of the children of Israel.

13 And the Egyptians made the children of Israel to serue with rigour.

Exodus 1:11–13, King James Bible (1611)

11 So they appointed over them tax collectors to afflict them with their burdens, and they built store cities for Pharaoh, namely Pithom and Raamses.

12 But as much as they would afflict them, so did they multiply and so did they gain strength, and they were disgusted because of the children of Israel.

13 So the Egyptians enslaved the children of Israel with back breaking labor.

Judaica Press Bible (translated by
Rabbi A. J. Rosenberg, 2005)

11 So they set gang-captains over it, to afflict it with their burdens. It built storage-cities for Pharaoh—-Pitom and Ra'amses.

12 But as they afflicted it, so did it become many, so did it burst forth. And they felt dread before the Children of Israel.

13 So they, Egypt, made the Children of Israel subservient with crushing-labor;

Schocken Bible (*The Five Books of Moses*,
translated by Everett Fox, 1997)

11 So they put overseers of forced work over them, in order to make their strength less by the weight of their work. And they made store-towns for Pharaoh, Pithom and Raamses.

12 But the more cruel they were to them, the more their number increased, till all the land was full of them. And the children of Israel were hated by the Egyptians.

13 And they gave the children of Israel even harder work to do:

Darby Bible (1890)

11 So the Egyptians put slave drivers over them to crush their spirits with hard labor. The Israelites built the cities of Pithom and Rameses to serve as supply centers for the king. 12 But the more the Egyptians oppressed the Israelites, the more they increased in number and the farther they spread through the land. The Egyptians came to fear the Israelites 13–14 and made their lives miserable by forcing them into cruel slavery.

Good News Bible: Today's English Version
(American Bible Society, 1992)

11 So they put slave masters over them to oppress them with forced labor, and they built Pithom and Rameses as store cities for Pharaoh. 12 But the more they were oppressed, the more they multiplied and spread; so the Egyptians came to dread the Israelites 13 and worked them ruthlessly.

New International Version (1973)

THE BODY IN THE BIBLE is often simply descriptive: a signpost of emotion or an indicator of location. But in bondage, the body is far more than that; it is property and it is pain. In Hebrew, the labor of slavery was literally a "breaking" labor. In English, this is flattened, just as the body and its metaphors have been smoothed down throughout many translations. In Hebrew, the beginning of slavery involves animalistic imagery that sears the soul; in English, this is toned way down, made much less disturbing, less cruel and visceral. Slavery in Egypt starts nice and easy in the King James translation, with a pleasant-sounding baby boom: "and the children of Israel were fruitful, and increased abundantly, and multiplied, and waxed exceeding mighty; and the land was filled with them," Exodus 1:7 reads. But in Hebrew, the passage is more ominous. The verb *vayishretzu*, which the King James Bible translates as "multiplied," is actually the far more unsettling "they multiplied like little animals." Even-Shoshan explains that the word *sheretz* refers to all small creatures who reproduce quickly and have numerous descendants, such as scorpions, frogs, and mice.

This animal-like rate of reproduction is a problem for the Egyptians. And so, in Exodus 1:10, the Egyptians say, in the King James Version, "Let us deal wisely with them." But that's probably too kind a translation; the word *nitchakma* means "let us outsmart them." What is happening here grammatically is a cohortative mode, which is present in Hebrew but not in English; the cohortative is the form used to encourage a group to take action.

There is a difference between "let us deal wisely" and "let us outsmart," though I can imagine how the King James translators got there, since the word *chochma*, "intelligence," and the word *nitchakma*, "let's outsmart," share a root.

And then comes Exodus 1:11 in the King James Bible, Authorized Version, Cambridge Edition:

> Therefore they did set ouer them taskmasters to afflict
> them with their burdens.

Taskmasters?

The 1611 King James Bible makes the same choice: "taskmasters."

But "taskmasters" is not what the literal Hebrew says. The Hebrew word means "tax masters."

Slavery in Hebrew begins with a tax. This tax, in Exodus 1:11, is a most unpleasant one. It is a tax so high it cannot be paid in money; it must be paid in bodily labor. This burden repeats throughout history—pay up or lose your freedom, your house, your right to reside, or worse, your life. There is a fascinating variety of translations of the words *sarei misim*, literally "tax masters" or "tax officers" in English. "Tax collectors" appears in a traditional Jewish translation from the Judaica Press, but Everett Fox opts for "gang-captains" in his Schocken translation. The New International translation has "slave masters" and the Good News translation goes with "slave drivers," and the 1890 Darby has "overseers of forced work." All of these are more emphatic than the King James's "taskmasters."

Perhaps the difference between "task" and "tax" is just an issue of clarity. After all, paying taxes is a task, an unpleasant one for most of us. The rabbis seem worried about clarity in their commentary on the beginnings of slavery, and they tend to overdo it when it comes to explaining what's going on.

Rashi looks at the word "taxes" in this passage and comments that the word "comes from the language of tax." Rashi was perhaps already worried that this word might be misunderstood. Then he clarifies further, and asks, "What is the tax? That they should build *arei miskenot*—meaning, cities of treasure—for Pharaoh."

I wondered whether swapping "tax" and "task" might be a modern problem, too. The dictionary Even-Shoshan says *sarei misim*, what the King James Bible translates as taskmasters, preside over *avodat k'fiyah*—forced labor. What matters here is the word "forced." Technically, these masters are "taskmasters," but the "tasks" are not voluntary, and forced labor or slave labor is much worse than a "task." Then as now, there is no business as profitable as unpaid labor. Someone is getting rich, even if the translation blurs both the financial and physical aspects of bondage. And it's easy to mistake what these "taskmasters" are doing in translation: in the King James Bible, they are there "to afflict them with their burdens."

The Hebrew is far harsher, far uglier. The taskmasters—or "gang-captains," as Everett Fox's Schocken translation puts it—are there not "to afflict," but to torture. A fascinating aspect of the word "torture" in Hebrew is that within it is the word for poverty. Then as now, poverty opens a person up to torture. The Hebrew doubles down, saying they were "tortured with their suffering." The rest of Exodus 1:11 is equally depressing, and equally tinged with finance. "And they built for Pharaoh treasure cities, Pithom and Raamses." Money's role in slavery can't be missed; the slaves made these cities strong, and fortified them to protect the loot. By Exodus 1:12, slavery is on in full force. But again, in English it doesn't sound that bad. The King James Bible says simply, "the more they afflicted them, the more they multiplied and grew." In Hebrew, the word is once again "tortured," not "afflicted." And in verse 13, the intersection of translation and morality—or immorality—is so egregious I laugh:

> And the Egyptians made the children of Israel to serve with rigor.

Rigor!

A literal translation would be: "And the Egyptians made the children of Israel work with breaking labor." That word for "breaking," *pharech*, comes from the verb *l'pharech*—meaning "to crush or crumble." The Egyptians focused on destroying the bodies of the Israelites, breaking them physically, getting as much out of their bodies as possible.

BUT JUST AS SLAVERY STARTS off softly with a baby boom, it is in the realm of birth, of maternal labor as opposed to slave labor, that things really get bad. And so, in Exodus 1:19, the King James Bible reads: "And the midwives said unto Pharaoh, because the Hebrew women are not as the Egyptian women: for they are lively, and are delivered ere the midwives come in unto them." The King James Bible does emphasize the Hebrews' otherness, which is always part of oppression—those creatures are not like us, they're different—but the passage loses something crucial in translation.

The midwives don't say that Jewish women are "lively"; they say they are *chayot*. In everyday modern Hebrew, *chayot* means "animals," and in the Bible, *chayot* often means "animals," too; therefore some commentators assume that the meaning here is that the Hebrew slaves were as "swift as animals" when they delivered their children. However, a close look at the word *chayot* here reveals that it is written a little differently, without a *dagesh*, the small dot that belongs inside the word. This tiny difference is a clue that the word, in this usage, may not mean "animals."

In the Talmud, the word *chayot* means "midwives," and this interpretation is adopted as well by the eleventh-century grammarian and lexicographer Ibn Janach. Here, perhaps reading *chayot* as "midwives" makes sense. The Hebrew women act as if they are midwives; they deliver their own children without help. And crucially, because they do so, the actual professional midwives are able to avoid Pharaoh's decree to kill all sons.

* * *

As the baby boom continues, so does slavery. In Exodus chapter 2, verse 23 in the King James Bible, "the children of Israel sighed by reason of the bondage, and they cried and their cry came up unto God by reason of the bondage."

In Hebrew the word does not mean "sighed," which sounds manageable, just as "rigor" does, but a "moaning," a "groaning." Professor Moshe Held, my mother's teacher, understood it not as groaning but as being exhausted. He based this on the Akkadian cognate. As for the word "cry," it's a shriek. Interestingly, a derivative of the Hebrew word that the King James Bible translates as "cry" has a new use in modern Hebrew. The word *haz'aka* means the piercing siren that stops the entire country twice a year—once to remember the Holocaust, and once to remember the war dead. It is also the word used for the warning siren when war breaks out or a terror attack occurs. The word choice is probably no accident.

Though the translators missed the siren sound, God hears it: what the King James Bible calls crying, and Rashi describes as shrieking. Its tone is the awful music of oppression. I wonder if it would have helped the abolitionist cause if all Bible readers in English could have sensed what God thought when God saw and heard slavery.

No elaboration is required in Exodus 2:24 and 2:25. Literally, the translation of 2:24 is "and God heard their groans and God remembered his covenant with Abraham and Isaac and Jacob." The siren cries of the slaves are so piercing that they force God to remember what he had promised. Then comes verse 25, which begins with the word *vayahr*, the same word used in creation to indicate that God is seeing, but also perhaps the word used to indicate understanding. The Hebrew is *vayahr elohim et b'nei yisrael vayeda elohim:* literally, "God saw the children of Israel, and God knew."

God got it. God understood what was going on. Just as "and God saw" succinctly indicates literal divine sight and something richer, something like understanding, so the phrase "and God knew" is simple and deep. It tells us that God was intimately familiar with what was happening to the Hebrew people in Egypt. But how can a devout, Bible-reading person understand how God felt about slavery when line 25 in the King James reads, "And God looked upon the children of Israel and God had respect unto them"?

There is no mention of respect in the Hebrew. The removal of "and God knew" and the addition of "and God had respect" enslaves us all in an incorrect translation of what slavery was like: for man and for God. There's no mention of respect anywhere in this chapter. There are just two words on God observing slavery—*vayeda elohim,* "and God knew." Perhaps the mistranslation of one word isn't consequential. But when a translation choice makes putting a human in permanent chains sound, well, just a little "rigorous," someone must cry out. Perhaps the way to break the idea that slavery is something "rigorous" that caused God to view the enslaved with "respect" is to break apart the translation, word by word, body part by body part, groan by groan, and shriek by piercing shriek.

GOD

A CLASSMATE WITH SPIKY HAIR WATCHES ME WRITE THE WORD *elohim* in Hebrew in my notebook, from right to left. For a moment she says nothing, and I can hear all the silence of Iowa. Then she taps my arm and in a whisper asks me to write God's name in her notebook, too, in Hebrew. My hand shakes as I nod.

I don't tell her she's asking me to transgress. The name of God is never written out by religious Jews. Instead, it's changed slightly, so that *elohim* becomes *elokim*. It's also pronounced that way during non-prayer uses, such as in a Bible class at a university. If I write God's name in my classmate's notebook, according to Jewish tradition she would never be able to throw her notebook out. She'd need to bury it. In Jewish tradition, any paper with God's name on it must be treated with respect, as if it were a part of a human body. But she isn't Jewish, so I know she is not bound by this rule.

I'm not concerned about my own pages; I already know I'm going to save my own notebook. So for her, I write *elokim*, then the letter *hey*—the *h* in *elohim*—separately. I'll explain after class. I will tell her it's God muted, as opposed to God at 200 proof.

Just then someone raises a hand and asks about "Yahweh."

In Hebrew the four letters that spell this version of God's name are completely unpronounceable, sort of like *cvxz*. Orthodox Jews just say Hashem, "the Name." No one I know from the Jewish community says Yahweh.

Someone else wants to talk about Yahweh, too. Everyone seems to want to discuss the name of God, as if there were only one name for God instead of many throughout the Torah.

Elohim, not *Yahweh*, is the name of God we are introduced to in Genesis 1:1, which reads, in Hebrew, *Bereishit bara elohim et hashamayim ve'et ha'aretz*, and which is often translated as "In the beginning God created the heavens and the earth." When the story of creation is retold in Genesis 2:4, God is referred to as *YKVK elohim* or *Yahweh elohim*, which a Hebrew reader would pronounce as *adonai* ("my lord") *elohim* ("my God"), though the *YKVK* is unpronounceable. The name is translated in the 1917 Jewish Publication Society translation as "the LORD God."

The meaning of *elohim* becomes even more complicated when we consider the grammar of it. The word is both a plural and a singular noun, like "deer" in English. But a multipart view of God is foreign to a Jewish reader steeped in the idea of one God, indivisible despite the multiplicity of names. The class moves quickly as I consider this. I struggle just to take notes.

SOMEONE READS ALOUD FROM THE beginning of Genesis: "The spirit of God moved over the water." "Spirit" is also a choice of translation, of how to read the word *ruach*, which literally means "wind." I wait for someone to ask "What is spirit?" Instead I hear talk of style, meaning, plot. Sweeping strokes—this is the first instinct of my classmates: to look at the big picture.

That's not the only way to read, however. I grew up with medieval thinkers battling over tiny points—one word, one letter, one vowel. In fact, my favorite commentator, Ibn Ezra, lays out five ways of studying the Torah, and the fifth and last is the path of grammar. I realize, listening only to the name of God and not to whether God is singular or plural, that grammar basically evaporates in translation. No one is asking why God's name is not *eloha*, the singular. No one asks whether it is possible that God is not singular but multiple in number.

Yet the twelfth-century commentator delves into the singular-plural question. Ibn Ezra has a beautiful explication on the use of *elohim* in Genesis 1:1. It is radical for a rabbi, especially one nine centuries ago, to even consider the possibility of multiple Gods—even if he eventually discredits the possibility, knocking it down, because the oneness of God is a central tenet of Judaism. Ibn Ezra says that it is only after we encounter the word *eloha* later in the text that we note that the word *elohim* in Genesis 1:1 is in the plural. Ibn Ezra does not offer a citation for where the word *eloha* appears, but it can be found in Deuteronomy 32:15, as well as in Isaiah, the Psalms, Job, Proverbs, and Daniel. In the 1917 Jewish Publication Society translation, Deuteronomy 32:15 reads: "But Jeshurun waxed fat, and kicked—thou didst wax fat, thou didst grow thick, thou didst become gross—and he forsook God who made him, and condemned the Rock of his salvation." That "forsook God who made him" is the famous phrase *vayitosh eloha asahu*, in which the word for God, *eloha*, is in the singular.

So why, then, is *elohim* in the plural in Genesis 1:1, when there is a singular word for God—*eloha*, the word used in Deuteronomy 32:15? Ibn Ezra then explains that "every language has a path of respect," such as the way a small child would address an adult. And in Hebrew, the path of respect is to address the great one—God—in the plural form. Biblical Hebrew isn't the only language that does this. Modern languages from French to Hindi use plural words like *vous* and *aap* as a form of respect.

The simplest example of this use of the plural in Hebrew is the word *adonai*, a word for God that appears in many prayers. The classic *baruch ata adonai* means "blessed are you our masters," with the word for "master" in the plural. *Adon*, or master, is the equivalent of "mister" in modern Hebrew; but in the plural, *adonai*, it refers to God. In the common blessing, *baruch*, "blessed," and *ata*, "you," are in the singular—indicating that God is also a singular being addressed with respect. Ibn Ezra notes that this plural-as-respected form occurs elsewhere in the Bible and offers two poetic examples. The first is the phrase *adonim kasheh*, which appears in Isaiah 19:4. In the 1917 Jewish Publication Society translation, the passage reads: "And I will give over the Egyptians into the hand of a cruel lord." This "cruel lord" is *adonim kasheh* in Hebrew, with *adonim* in the plural—literally, plural "masters"— but the *kasheh*, literally meaning "hard" but here translated figuratively as "cruel," is in the singular form. It is understood that this phrase, a mixture of plural and singular, refers to a respected singular God.

The clincher for Ibn Ezra is the form of the verb that follows the name of God. He points out that the verb *bara*, "created," is singular, not plural. So the meaning of Genesis 1:1, Ibn Ezra concludes, is that the name of God is singular, but in a respected form.

BACK IN IOWA MY TEACHER changes direction to discuss the broader goals of the course.

"To make the Bible accessible to you—to make you used to it."

I write this down.

"To talk about it as literature."

I write that, too.

"It's a very great literature, with as much influence as anything," she says next.

She is devout—I can hear it—and she is a major literary writer.

It is hard to be both an artist and a person of faith: how lucky I am to have her to read with me. I used to think the conflict between believing in God and making art was a particularly poignant problem for Jews, many of whom believe that the line from Exodus 20:4—"Thou shalt not make unto thee a graven image, nor any manner of likeness, of anything that is in heaven above, or that is in the earth beneath, or that is in the water under the earth," in the 1917 Jewish Publication Society translation—applies to any human being who attempts to create a work of art. In Hebrew, the word *pesel*, translated as "graven image," is the modern Hebrew word for sculpture. The next word, *t'muna*, translated here as "any manner of likeness," is the modern Hebrew word for a painting. This passage from Exodus has haunted Jewish visual artists who grew up in observant homes, including the artist Marc Chagall, who actually hired a beggar to pose as his father praying—in his father's prayer shawl and *tefillin*, or phylacteries. One of those paintings is in the Art Institute of Chicago, and I like to go look at it. Chagall wrote that he painted the image because he felt the need to capture a way of life that was dying out. I imagine he thought his own father would never agree to sit for him.

I used to feel that the verse was a direct challenge not only for the Jewish visual artist but for the writer, too, those of us who insist on inventing images with words, creating characters, making people live on the page as God makes them live in the world. A writer who has labored on a character for a long time can feel a love for the invented being, perhaps a love not far from what the idol worshipper feels toward the god he has made with his own hands. But the conflict between art and faith is not, I have gradually decided, just a Jewish issue. It is not about that line between graven images and an unseeable God. Instead, it is the very idea of belief that is a problem for a devoted artist. Belief implies acceptance. An artist is different—a questioner in the heart, not necessarily a believer. An artist does not accept first and do next, as the Jewish people supposedly did at Sinai. An artist is a—

"Supercessionism," my teacher says, jolting me from my thoughts. "What is that?" I ask.

"The Christian habit of treating the old as subordinate," she says.

Isaiah in second place? Moses as runner-up?

I wonder about the Christian habit, and then about the Jewish habit of treating the old as infinitely better, always.

My teacher's comments stick in my mind. A few months later, I read one of my father's favorite books, *The Lonely Man of Faith*, written in the 1960s by Rabbi Joseph B. Soloveitchik, known as the Rav. The Rav came from the Litvak line of rabbis—Talmudic scholars descended intellectually from the line of the Vilna Gaon, or the genius of Vilna. The Rav, in other words, was from *misnagdim* royalty, from the pinnacle of "objector" scholarship, meaning those who "objected" to Chassidism, the eighteenth-century movement that insisted that belief and emotion mattered above all, above scholarship and rational thought. The "objectors," including Soloveitchik, strenuously objected to that idea. Knowledge matters, they insisted.

But the Rav did not have an entirely hard-line, intellectual education. From an early age, he experienced other worlds. As a child, the Rav had a Chassidic teacher, and from this teacher he learned something about feeling—and perhaps love. The Rav, though certainly not a Chassid himself, wrote that God had ordained that there should be Chassidim as well as *misnagdim* in the world.

"It was very daring of him to say that," my father likes to say. I often hear daring in the Rav's writing.

The Rav, it turns out, in the 1965 essay that became *Lonely Man*, is interested in what my classmate with the spiky hair is interested in: the name of God. He points out that there are two creation stories in Hebrew, two versions of Adam and Eve. And in the second, God is referred to as Yahweh, not as *elohim*.

The name of God, as God is identified in the first verse of Genesis, is not static. The Rav writes that God changes his own name in his next creation version. Here, it might be helpful to explain that as an Orthodox rabbi, the Rav probably believed that God himself was the author of the Bible. As a child, I was taught that God dictated and Moses wrote the words down, which is certainly not what Bible scholars in major universities tell their students. The Rav was a towering scholar who earned a Ph.D. in philosophy in Germany, and his essay is full of surprising references to the Greek Septuagint and the Latin Vulgate. But he was also very much, and very deeply, a man of faith. He was aware of the conflict inherent in this, of the strangeness of thinking critically and believing in God's dominion at the same time. And so the Rav finds, in Genesis, two competing strands in man, and in man's relationship with God.

In version one, "Adam the first," as the Rav refers to him, is commanded to dominate the earth. This Adam is the creative, strong man who builds spaceships, writes theorems, and composes poetry. God gives this busy man a helpmate, Eve, to assist him in getting everything done. Version two presents a man who "emerges alone," who has had part of him removed to make Eve. This Adam wants to submit to God, and to have a deep spiritual communion with Eve in order to survive on earth. The man of faith, according to the Rav, is lonely, because he is always caught between these two opposites: the desire to create, to master the earth, to dominate, and the desire to submit to divinity, to ask why, to know always that he is incomplete—that there is another above.

So the man of faith is always at war with himself.

Sitting in the classroom in Iowa, thinking about the name of God, I am not rebelling against tradition but following a long history that believes that to truly understand anything you must duke it out, on the inside, both with yourself and with God.

MY MOTHER TAUGHT ME THAT language is not simply words; it is an opening into a way of thinking, a view of the world, a naming of its neighborhoods. But it is not easy to make a language come alive for someone who does not speak that language; it is a challenge to rename the seemingly familiar and name the unfamiliar. The effort often results in clumsiness and misunderstanding. Perhaps this is why translators are often reviled.

The Italians say *traduttore-traditore:* translator-traitor. The great Hebrew poet Chaim Nachman Bialik memorably described translation as a "kiss through a handkerchief." The American poet Robert Frost reportedly said that "poetry is what is lost in translation." But the view of some rabbis on the Septuagint, the translation of the Bible into Greek, is worse—that it should be marked by a fast. The Megilat Ta'anit Batra, an ancient pre-Mishnaic scroll of the holidays, lists a fast on the anniversary of the publication of the Septuagint, noting: "On the eighth of Tevet, in the days of King Ptolemy, the Torah was written in Greek and darkness descended on the world for three days."

The Talmud has several takes on the story of the Septuagint, the first translation of the Hebrew Bible, which was commissioned by the Greek-speaking Jewish community of Alexandria, Egypt, in the third century B.C.E., because the community was afraid that Jews could no longer read Hebrew. Some versions focus on the changes between the Hebrew and the Greek, though in fact there are many more changes than the Talmud notes. In one of the Talmud's versions of the story, a legend related in Bavli Megilla 9a, King Ptolemy decided he wanted a Greek translation of the Torah, and he therefore ordered seventy-two scholars into separate rooms, without telling them why they were there. He then went to each of them and said, "Translate for me the Torah of Moses." Miraculously—"God put an idea into the heart of each one"—all seventy-two translators produced the exact same translation.

But just a few centuries after the Septuagint, Greek was going out of style, too. The language of the streets at that time was Aramaic; and so the next major Jewish translation of the Bible was the Targum—literally, "translation," but referring to the translation into Aramaic. As I looked at the Aramaic and then at the English, I often thought about that idea of darkness descending over the world for days, because it sometimes seemed that disaster followed me as long as I read the Bible in translation.

I PROBABLY HELPED CREATE SOME of the disaster by moving too often. I moved dozens of times after starting college in Baltimore: I spent eight months in Paris as a student at the Sorbonne, then returned to Baltimore to graduate, then tried New York, as a copy editor and reporter on Wall Street at a daily newspaper covering the bond market. Within two years I was in Boston for graduate school in poetry; then, as soon as school ended, I did a stint in Germany on a fellowship cosponsored by the German government and Hillel called "Bridges of Understanding," then went back to Boston, where I set up shop as a freelance journalist. I began to split my working life between covering finance and covering culture, and the mix left me time to learn as much as I could about poetry. In Boston, in 1999 and 2000, I had an idyllic living situation with a close friend who was starting a career as a painter. Surrounded by her paintings, I was able to convince myself that a life of art was possible. Perhaps we convinced each other that it could be done.

In 2000, my friend got a fellowship to graduate school, and I moved to Jerusalem, where I wrote a travel column and spent much of my time on the road; then back to New York again, briefly, and then a move across the country to Iowa City, where, for a time, all was quiet.

But once I had my degree in hand, I was back to the road; back to New York, then California, then back to Iowa—and finally to Chicago. In between I trekked to Europe whenever I had the time and the money. I would get exhausted filing several state tax forms each year, year in and year out; in fact, I feel tired just typing out my many moves. In the four years after finishing graduate school in 2005, until I finally settled in one apartment in Chicago, with a mesmerizing view of the water that gives me the illusion that yes, I am still traveling, yes, I am still close to the edge of the earth, the pace of my moves increased from once a year, minimum, to several times a year. The more I tried to remain in place, the less I did so, though I learned a lot from the moving, as I suppose most nomads do.

In one of the highlights of the move-a-thon, I found myself living with a rock band in Chicago for a few months, and for a summer with four guys ranging in age from twenty-two to sixty in California. My particular living space in Berkeley was nicknamed "the Jack Kerouac Cabin," and the landlord, a professor of drama who became another dear friend, spoke French and was fond of cooking Moroccan food—*tajines*—in an earthenware pot he had purchased in Morocco just for this purpose. He was incredibly comfortable with youth and with dreams. Later, I lived for a few months in an apartment in Chicago that I nicknamed "Republican Heaven": the nice young man who sublet it to me went off to join McCain's presidential campaign, but he left his Rudy Giuliani hot sauce in the kitchen.

THE MOVES ALL BEGAN AROUND the time I hurt my hand. I write by hand, and had been doing so for years; I had been writing seriously since I was eighteen. Then, when I was just past thirty, my hand hurt so much I could not sit without aspirin. And it was about to get much worse; I could not use my right hand for a year and a half after that because of the immense pain, which a doctor who specialized in hands told me came from the simplest of causes: overuse.

He called in another physician, from the navy, just to show him my hand. "You will not see this again in your career," he said to the other physician. "Take a close look. This is an injury from fifty, a hundred years ago, from old men who used their hands nonstop."

It was a malady of scribes and translators, the pain of rabbis and old-time newspaper reporters scribbling on paper pads. My hand was a throwback to a prior era.

The doctor prescribed time, a resting of the hands.

Then he said, "Have you heard of this thing? It's a great invention. It's called a computer."

All I could do was wait. During the worst of it, a friend would come over to feed me. I stopped cooking dinner after the physical therapist said: *Do you want to chop vegetables or write poetry?* I got over it through a magic potion of daily swimming and time, and probably luck, but I certainly saw what for a writer is darkness: the possibility that she might not be able to write.

Scared by the severity of the pain, I changed the rhythm of my life. I made the prudent-seeming but probably foolish decision to switch from freelancing to taking a steady corporate job. Those were some of the worst months I have experienced, despite the salary, the suits, the gleaming glass building. I longed for the tremendous freedom I had had, the vast liberty of the page, of control over my own destiny.

Eventually, I decided to walk out of corporate America and just write.

I HAD EXACTLY THREE WEEKS between quitting my job and breaking my foot falling down a single stair at a museum in San Francisco.

I could not walk for a year.

This time, too, I encountered a fantastic doctor, about a week after the emergency room physician said I just needed to rest for three days. This doctor played opera music for me for over an hour, during which he said nothing. The arias were heartbreakingly sad.

"I am playing this for you to make sure you understand how serious your situation is," the doctor said. "You have broken twelve bones. Listen carefully to what I am saying.

"You must take this seriously. If you decide to hop to a coffee shop, it's over. If you do not rest, completely, for as long as possible, you may never walk again."

I tried not to shudder.

"It is sad when a young woman loses a year of her life," he

said. "But remember, the risk of walking too early is that you may never walk normally again. My advice is stay in your apartment and go nowhere."

Then the doctor delivered this clincher. "My father survived the gulag," he told me, "and you will survive this."

He drove me home. Next, he insisted that I see the top surgeon, even though he thought I would not need surgery, just a lot of time. He showed up to my appointment with her, where they wheeled me into an MRI, with possible surgery on the horizon, only to find out that all of my bones were swollen.

I had no idea bones could swell.

The pain was excruciating. Tears slipped down my face at all hours; I had never experienced such searing, pointy pain, like that of a knife cutting, back and forth, across my foot. After a week of looking out onto the hills of San Francisco from the window, and depending on others for the delivery of basics, I decided that while it was a lot prettier than what I'd see in the gulag, I was not sure I could survive a year like this.

My friends and my landlady helped with a move out of my apartment, and I moved in with my parents again. I flew across the country with my foot elevated, sitting between two kind men: the head of the physics department at a major university, who explained the importance of elevation in my condition, and a retired pilot, who explained what flight does to the body, and how I should not be afraid.

"Altitude makes it swell," he said. "Don't panic."

It was my right foot. I could not walk, I could not drive, and my right arm—which I needed for crutches—was still recovering from overwriting. "Darkness descended," I thought, trying to make chocolate work as well as Vicodin to avoid adding addiction to the mix. I spent that Passover with my foot raised on eight pillows. When my sister got married, I was in a boot, unable to wear elegant shoes, or to dance. And I remembered what an older man in Iowa City said to me about the whole idea of a Jewish girl reading the Christian Bible.

When I first bought the Oxford Annotated Bible, the first English-language Bible I ever owned, I carried it around in a brown paper bag. I grew up with the concept of *marit ayin*, or how things look to the eye, meaning the naked eye; for example, a person who keeps kosher might not go into a burger joint to buy a coffee, even though black coffee is definitely kosher. Walking around with the Old and New Testament doesn't look like a Jewish activity; it looks suspiciously unkosher. A person passing by might not understand. The first place I went in Iowa City with my brown paper bag happened to be Hillel, the Jewish student center, and an older man I met there, who saw the Oxford peeking out—we were both volunteering our time—commented that he was sure I had better things to do than to read the Torah in a Christian translation.

"It's not a good book for you," he said quietly.

The older man was echoing the Talmud's warning about the very idea of the Torah in a language other than Hebrew. The concern is simple: The translation will be used to convert Jews to Christianity. It will be used against the Jewish people, as in fact it has been for hundreds of years. It will introduce you to the idea of a Moses with horns.

That conversation—that warning—"It's not a good book for you"—came back to me as I traveled. In Rome, I looked up at the sky and realized the Jewish ghetto was hemmed in by a church. I read that Jewish children, kidnapped by the church, would then lead their parents to conversion: the only other choice, for the parents, was never to see their children again. As I spent more

time in Europe, imagining the lives of the biblical commentators, I realized the shadow the church cast over the lives of these
medieval rabbis: they lived in fear of death. At any moment, they
could be cast out of their homes, or given a choice—convert or
die. The lucky ones got the choice to flee, and this fleeing explains
why there are Jews all over the world.

The call to conversion is a major part of many other faiths; a
faith that does not push conversion is always at risk. The rabbis
of the Talmudic era had seen the Roman Empire's efforts to pro-
mote an abandonment of Judaism, but they could not have known
what would follow: the Crusades, the infamous blood libels, the
pogroms that cost thousands of Jews their lives, from Germany to
Russia. My mother's cousin lives on a street in Israel called Me-
nachem Beilis: it is named after one of the victims of a blood libel,
but most of the victims' names have been long forgotten.

But Christians who worked to translate the Bible from Hebrew also risked death. It was perhaps not a good book for them,
either. They, too, were victims of the world's suspicion of people
who bridge languages and traverse worlds. The lives and deaths
of Christian biblical translators are a cautionary tale of darkness.

William Tyndale (c. 1494–1536), the first to use Hebrew and
Greek versions as he translated into English, was tried for heresy,
strangled, and burned at the stake in 1536. His crime was the
very act of translation. Having a version of the Bible in English—
the vernacular—was considered a challenge to both the Roman
Catholic Church and English laws to maintain church rulings.
Tyndale, a Lutheran, must have known how dangerous his work
was; he had to leave England and go to Germany to learn Hebrew. It was not just church law that probably motivated Tyndale

to go elsewhere; England had expelled all its Jews in 1290, so it seems reasonable to assume that it would have been difficult for Tyndale to access Jewish scholarship on the Bible if he remained in England. At the time, the idea that ordinary people would be able to read the Bible in their own language, and to make their own decisions about what it meant, was viewed as a threatening possibility, as clerical letters from the time demonstrate. In *William Tyndale: A Biography*, David Daniell addresses why Tyndale was imprisoned and condemned: "In other words, the charge was heresy, with not agreeing with the Holy Roman Emperor—in a nutshell, being a Lutheran."

But the hounding of translators preceded Tyndale. John Wycliffe led an effort to translate the Latin Vulgate—the translation completed in 405 by Jerome, who worked from the Hebrew—directly into the English vernacular in 1382. Wycliffe managed to die naturally, of a stroke, in 1384, but his remains were exhumed in 1428, burned to ashes, and thrown into the River Swift.

Translation must have mattered, if that kind of treatment kept occurring. For centuries, translating a text signified that it was essential, that someone thought it was worth preserving. The story of the Bible in translation is far wider than just Hebrew and English, or Hebrew and Aramaic, or Hebrew and Greek and Latin. In the tenth century, the major scholar Rabbi Sa'adiah Gaon, who was the head of the Torah Academy of Sura, in ancient Babylon, translated the entire Torah into Arabic, because in his time, Arabic was the language most spoken by the Jewish community. Perhaps Sa'adiah, too, feared that the Bible might die without his immediate action. The translators of old, working by hand, carrying books, running from authorities near and far, gave both their hands and their feet to history, to the love of a book—or so I told myself as I tried to rest.

* * *

SOMETIMES THE LOVE, I MUST admit, goes too far. In the Harold Washington Library in Chicago, the main branch of the Chicago Public Library, when I ask to see a copy of the 1850 edition of Wycliffe's translation of Jerome's Vulgate, which I can't seem to find, the librarian casually mentions that it's not unusual for the edition not to be where it's supposed to be.

"Bibles and religious books are our most stolen texts," she says. "Every library I've ever worked at—and there have been many—has had Bible stealers."

She writes down for me the library's hours for special collections and also the address of the Newberry Library, a twenty-minute walk away, where she thinks I might find it. She tells me the University of Chicago has one, too, or so the catalog says—but catalogs, she insists, don't mean anything.

"Be sure to call first, to check that the Bibles are where they are supposed to be," she says.

That night, as on so many nights, I read the words of the rabbis and imagine their conversations. In the classic text *Pirkei Avot*, or Ethics of the Fathers, they ask: *Eizehu chacham?* (Who is wise?) "He who learns from every human being," they answer. *Eizehu ashir?* (Who is wealthy?) "He who is happy with his lot."

Some of these rabbis' statements have been set to music. The way of the Torah, I sang as a child in the school chorus, is to eat bread and salt, sleep on the earth, lead a life of sorrow, and labor in the learning of the Torah. Every time I sing that song to myself, I wonder if I agree with it—with this idea of study as labor. The reading of the Bible is a struggle, but it is also a pleasure. It has always been like this: a joy and a war. And it's not like manual labor. It is hard but also energizing. For me, it is not a life of sorrow.

* * *

My great-grandfather Moshe, who lived in Bremen, Germany, used to come home at ten or eleven at night, after a long day of selling dry goods from a pack on his back, and sit and read the Talmud. My grandfather described his father's nightly ritual to me just once, near the end of his life. There was an unloading off the back and then a glass of water and then reading.

"Imagine how exhausted he must have been," my grandfather said, "and he just began reading."

I imagined. I have seen exactly one photograph of the man.

"He didn't sleep right away, after such a long day, his whole business on his back," my grandfather said. "Night is when he *started* studying."

I was foolish not to ask more questions when I could.

Instead, I imagine: my grandfather as a boy, learning Isaiah, coming across the Malbim's explanation that man contains the angel of God and also the sword. It is one of my favorite moments in Isaiah commentary. The Malbim, an acronym for Meïr Leibush ben Jehiel Michel Weiser, wandered throughout his life, and was even thrown in jail in the mid-1800s by his own congregants for his refusal to adapt to modernity, his insistence on clinging to Orthodox Judaism and its texts. I imagine that my great-grandfather Moshe, a devout Chassidic man living in Germany, a country in which most Jews in the early twentieth century were assimilated and where the more liberal Reform Judaism was born, might have taught his son the commentary of a rabbi like the Malbim, who railed against change and clung to tradition with his fingernails.

It was not a popular stance, and it got the Malbim put into prison. He was eventually released from jail with the help of the wealthy Sir Moses Montefiore, but with the condition that he

leave Romania. Then the Malbim actually went to Constantino-
ple to ask the Turkish government for help in his battle against
his congregation. Jewish history is all about that: one idea battling another, and one unusual thinker pressing on, despite the
dangers.

Maybe that's why the idea that there is some connection between potential bodily harm and translation intrigues me. The
Megilat Ta'anit Batra, a calendar of fast days, lists a fast on the
anniversary of the publication of the Septuagint, and as the various disasters kept happening to me as I read through the King
James Bible—the injured hand, the broken foot—I wondered if
the Talmud was onto something.

I imagine Wycliffe, shivering as he translated in frigid Europe: poor man, he had no aspirin, no heat but fire, nothing to
help him forget that his body was suffering for the Bible.

I UNDERSTAND THE ALEXANDRIANS' FEAR that Hebrew might die
out. Most Jews in America are secular, but even in the religious
community, I have encountered observant Jews who know very
little Hebrew. This past Yom Kippur, someone tapped my shoul-
der: it was a woman in a wig, asking me to help her find the Torah reading. She was embarrassed not to know what the passage
was, but I was worried about the wider picture, the communal
future. I can understand that the Alexandrians felt they needed
to do something, and fast, to protect the Torah from extinction.

Perhaps this fear is what drives my mother to give Hebrew
classes at all hours of the day, and late at night, to make sure both
working adults and students can understand Hebrew grammar.
Perhaps this is why the Jewish Publication Society committee met
and worked through disagreements, which I imagine turned quite

spirited. This fear is probably what Sa'adiah Gaon must have had in mind, translating the Torah into Arabic. He probably thought Arabic had a fighting chance of survival; Hebrew, not so much.

IT IS INCREDIBLE THAT HEBREW, alone among all the ancient languages, was revived. That surprise is the unexpected subtext of the story of biblical translation: for twenty-two hundred years, there has been an effort to translate Hebrew texts because no one expected Hebrew to live again, as it has. The medieval translators and commentators couldn't imagine that, surrounded as they were by the threat of Crusades, the string of expulsions, the violent strains of Islam. Every European country I have visited in my efforts to understand the commentators' lives has gone through a period in which its entire Jewish population was expelled. The commentators were used to fighting for their lives.

But they also fought to preserve a legacy of reading—a conversation that had gone on for thousands of years. They quoted earlier rabbis, arguing with them but most importantly helping their ideas live on. I eventually realized I would have to fight, too, if I wanted to convey a centuries-old conversation in English. I learned to write through physical pain, for months, then years. Throughout my constant moves I tried to stretch cash for as far as it would go, trying to master the equation between money and time. I learned to travel at the absolute cheapest times, in the dead of winter, to explore cities that once mattered to the biblical commentators but that are reachable today only by occasional noisy local trains. Several times, I grew so exasperated with the difficulty of structuring the space between languages that I put the project away. The whole thing was taking too long, and it was too messy, too risky. Each word and phrase in the Bible was a minefield of potential mistakes. Every millimeter of text had been combed by scholars for centuries.

Sometimes the absurdity of what I was doing hit me. How could I express the difference between an ancient language and a modern one and have it make any sense? In California, looking out at the flowers from the window of my cabin—really, a converted garage—I realized I had spent an entire summer trying to write the grammatical mystery of Genesis 1:1 and 1:2. Worse still, I had previously spent several months in the late winter and the spring writing that same thing. What was that—a year, on two verses? Darkness fell over me as I realized the summer was gone.

For a while I did anything but write. I went to the theater, I visited museums, I joined a wonderful lay-led synagogue in the Mission District, all song and dance and happy radicalism. I tried to live a life. Then I realized that there is darkness in avoiding your task. The rabbis are right: it may not be your obligation to finish the task, but neither are you free to shirk it. Perhaps darkness is just a beginning, what must come before creation. And so I returned to what had begun in Iowa: the reading of the Bible in English and the writing about it. I took out all my notes, all my drafts, and worked at making them as clear as I possibly could, starting with the word *elohim*, as God is referred to in the first line of Genesis.

It felt like day one, beginning all over again.

I was embarrassed at how long the project was taking. I would experience that—the leaving the project, the darkness, and then the returning to it—many more times after that. Sometimes, reading one commentator attacking another, I thought their vehemence must have mirrored the war within themselves: their doubt about whether their own commentary meant anything at all. Reading so much about God reminds a human reader of her limitations, and of the difference between the human and the divine.

Still, the struggle with God, and the Bible's willingness to depict it, is what keeps bringing me back to my stacks of Bibles. I am moved again by Moses initially refusing God's call, and by Sarah laughing at the idea that God will give her a son, and by Jacob wrestling with the angel. It is a story that is part of every man and woman who has ever felt the need to claw against destiny, to insist on a different future than what God appears to be offering. And sometimes, in the Bible, what man wants so passionately is unacceptable to God. What man wants is so destructive that it is a threat to the earth, to the creatures that live on it, to other humans. Then there is another round in the battle, a round of definite statements of what man may and may not do. God has an additional punch to throw; in those cases, the result of that man-God wrestling match becomes law.

LAW

מֹשֶׁה אֶת־דִּבְרֵי הָעָם אֶל־יְהֹוָה: וַיֹּאמֶר יְהֹוָה אֶל־מֹשֶׁה י

לֵךְ אֶל־הָעָם וְקִדַּשְׁתָּם הַיּוֹם וּמָחָר וְכִבְּסוּ שִׂמְלֹתָם: וְהָיוּ 11

נְכֹנִים לַיּוֹם הַשְּׁלִישִׁי כִּי ׀ בַּיּוֹם הַשְּׁלִשִׁי יֵרֵד יְהֹוָה לְעֵינֵי

כָל־הָעָם עַל־הַר סִינָי: וְהִגְבַּלְתָּ אֶת־הָעָם סָבִיב לֵאמֹר 12

הִשָּׁמְרוּ לָכֶם עֲלוֹת בָּהָר וּנְגֹעַ בְּקָצֵהוּ כָּל־הַנֹּגֵעַ בָּהָר

מוֹת יוּמָת: לֹא־תִגַּע בּוֹ יָד כִּי־סָקוֹל יִסָּקֵל אוֹ־יָרֹה יִיָּרֶה 13

אִם־בְּהֵמָה אִם־אִישׁ לֹא יִחְיֶה בִּמְשֹׁךְ הַיֹּבֵל הֵמָּה יַעֲלוּ

בָהָר: וַיֵּרֶד מֹשֶׁה מִן־הָהָר אֶל־הָעָם וַיְקַדֵּשׁ אֶת־הָעָם 14

וַיְכַבְּסוּ שִׂמְלֹתָם: וַיֹּאמֶר אֶל־הָעָם הֱיוּ נְכֹנִים לִשְׁלֹשֶׁת טו

יָמִים אַל־תִּגְּשׁוּ אֶל־אִשָּׁה: וַיְהִי בַיּוֹם הַשְּׁלִישִׁי בִּהְיֹת 16

הַבֹּקֶר וַיְהִי קֹלֹת וּבְרָקִים וְעָנָן כָּבֵד עַל־הָהָר וְקֹל שֹׁפָר

חָזָק מְאֹד וַיֶּחֱרַד כָּל־הָעָם אֲשֶׁר בַּמַּחֲנֶה: וַיּוֹצֵא מֹשֶׁה 17

אֶת־הָעָם לִקְרַאת הָאֱלֹהִים מִן־הַמַּחֲנֶה וַיִּתְיַצְּבוּ בְּתַחְתִּית

הָהָר: וְהַר סִינַי עָשַׁן כֻּלּוֹ מִפְּנֵי אֲשֶׁר יָרַד עָלָיו יְהֹוָה 18

בָּאֵשׁ וַיַּעַל עֲשָׁנוֹ כְּעֶשֶׁן הַכִּבְשָׁן וַיֶּחֱרַד כָּל־הָהָר מְאֹד:

וַיְהִי קוֹל הַשֹּׁפָר הוֹלֵךְ וְחָזֵק מְאֹד מֹשֶׁה יְדַבֵּר וְהָאֱלֹהִים 19

יַעֲנֶנּוּ בְקוֹל: וַיֵּרֶד יְהֹוָה עַל־הַר סִינַי אֶל־רֹאשׁ הָהָר *aa.*

וַיִּקְרָא יְהֹוָה לְמֹשֶׁה אֶל־רֹאשׁ הָהָר וַיַּעַל מֹשֶׁה: וַיֹּאמֶר 21

יְהֹוָה אֶל־מֹשֶׁה רֵד הָעֵד בָּעָם פֶּן־יֶהֶרְסוּ אֶל־יְהֹוָה לִרְאוֹת

וְנָפַל מִמֶּנּוּ רָב: וְגַם הַכֹּהֲנִים הַנִּגָּשִׁים אֶל־יְהֹוָה יִתְקַדָּשׁוּ 22

פֶּן־יִפְרֹץ בָּהֶם יְהֹוָה: וַיֹּאמֶר מֹשֶׁה אֶל־יְהֹוָה לֹא־יוּכַל 23

הָעָם לַעֲלֹת אֶל־הַר סִינָי כִּי־אַתָּה הַעֵדֹתָה בָּנוּ לֵאמֹר

הַגְבֵּל אֶת־הָהָר וְקִדַּשְׁתּוֹ: וַיֹּאמֶר אֵלָיו יְהֹוָה לֶךְ־רֵד 24

וְעָלִיתָ אַתָּה וְאַהֲרֹן עִמָּךְ וְהַכֹּהֲנִים וְהָעָם אַל־יֶהֶרְסוּ

לַעֲלֹת אֶל־יְהֹוָה פֶּן־יִפְרָץ־בָּם: וַיֵּרֶד מֹשֶׁה אֶל־הָעָם כה

וַיֹּאמֶר אֲלֵהֶם: ס

CAP. XX. כ

ב

וַיְדַבֵּר אֱלֹהִים אֵת כָּל־הַדְּבָרִים הָאֵלֶּה לֵאמֹר: ס אָנֹכִי א 2

יהוה

1 The ten Commandements. 18 The people are afraid. 20 Moses comforteth them. 22 Idolatrie is forbidden. 24 Of what sort the Altar should be.

1 And God spake all these words, saying,

2 I am the Lord thy God, which haue brought thee out of the land of Egypt, out of the house of bondage.

3 Thou shalt haue no other Gods before me.

4 Thou shalt not make vnto thee any grauen Image, or any likenesse of any thing that is in heauen aboue, or that is in the earth beneath, or that is in the water vnder the earth.

5 Thou shalt not bow downe thy selfe to them, nor serue them: For I the Lord thy God am a iealous God, visiting the iniquitie of the fathers vpon the children, vnto the thirde and fourth generation of them that hate me:

6 And shewing mercy vnto thousands of them that loue mee, and keepe my Commandements.

7 Thou shalt not take the Name of the Lord thy God in vaine: for the Lord will not holde him guiltlesse, that taketh his Name in vaine.

8 Remember the Sabbath day, to keepe it holy.

9 Six dayes shalt thou labour, and doe all thy worke:

10 But the seuenth day is the Sabbath of the Lord thy God: in it thou shalt not doe any worke, thou, nor thy sonne, nor thy daughter, thy man seruant, nor thy mayd seruant, nor thy cattell, nor thy stranger that is within thy gates:

11 For in six dayes the Lord made heauen and earth, the sea, and all that in them is, and rested the seuenth day: wherefore the Lord blessed the Sabbath day, and halowed it.

12 Honour thy father and thy mother: that thy dayes may bee long vpon the land, which the Lord thy God giueth thee.

13 Thou shalt not kill.

14 Thou shalt not commit adultery.

15 Thou shalt not steale.

16 Thou shalt not beare false witnes against thy neighbour.

17 Thou shalt not couet thy neighbours house, thou shalt not couet thy neighbours wife, nor his man seruant, nor his maid seruant, nor his oxe, nor his asse, nor any thing that is thy neighbours.

18 And all the people saw the thundrings, and the lightnings, and the noise of the trumpet, and the mountaine smoking: and when the people saw it, they remooued, and stood a farre off.

19 And they saide vnto Moses, Speake thou with vs, and wee will heare: But let not God speake with vs, lest we die.

20 And Moses said vnto the people, Feare not: for God is come to prooue you, and that his feare may bee before your faces, that ye sinne not.

21 And the people stood afarre off, and Moses drew neere vnto the thicke darkenes, where God was.

22 And the Lord said vnto Moses, Thus thou shalt say vnto the children of Israel, Yee haue seene that I haue talked with you from heauen.

23 Ye shall not make with me gods of siluer, neither shall ye make vnto you gods of gold.

24 An Altar of earth thou shalt make vnto me, and shalt sacrifice thereon thy burnt offerings, and thy peace offerings, thy sheepe, and thine oxen: In all places where I record my Name, I will come vnto thee, and I will blesse thee.

25 And if thou wilt make mee an Altar of stone, thou shalt not build it of hewen stone: for if thou lift vp thy toole vpon it, thou hast polluted it.

26 Neither shalt thou goe vp by steps vnto mine Altar, that thy nakednesse be not discouered thereon.

Exodus 20:1–26, King James Bible (1611)

———————◆———————

"MOSAIC LAW CAN BE HARSH," MARILYNNE ROBINSON SAID to the class one day, and I looked up in surprise. First of all—what was "Mosaic law"?

Jewish law, as practiced today, comes from the Mishna and the Talmud, written by rabbis who lived many centuries after Moses. The laws codified by the Mishna, themselves the result of about two hundred years of debate, are further enveloped by volumes of discussion and argument, written down in the Talmud. The Talmud is part of what is called *Torah sh'be'al peh*, or Oral Law. The law in the Torah itself is not considered the final word; instead, Orthodox Jews accept both the Torah law, or written law, and the Oral Law. Without the commentary of the rabbis, perhaps parts of "Mosaic law" do seem harsh. But no one who grew up immersed in Jewish text understands "an eye for an eye" to mean an actual eye for an actual eye. Instead, the idea is to take something equivalent to the harm, which generally means a monetary punishment.

But the whole mention of "Mosaic law" and its "harshness" makes me think that reading the Bible in translation is not just a matter of language. The Hebrew Bible is a lived text, and in the community I grew up in, it was never read alone. Instead, the Bible is part of a constellation of texts; Jewish law, too, comes not only from the Bible itself, but from the various texts *discussing* what the Bible actually means. Conversation, then, is an integral part of law, even to Jews who believe the Bible is the word of God dictated to Moses.

While I am thinking about this issue, I go back to my high school to hear an alumnus, who is now a law professor, give a talk on what makes Jewish law different from other types of law. He points out that in Roman law, the emperor decided what was right. In British law, the king decided what was right. But in Jewish law, the king is not allowed into the court of law; there is a barrier between law and power. Beyond that, the power to decide exactly what a law means is given to human beings, so Jewish law is necessarily flawed, being human, and not a thing of God. It is something that people discuss. The professor also says that he views the weekly reading of the Torah as a weekly reading of the law, so that every listener can familiarize himself with the law instead of just the judges. It all sounds very public to me. And if a system of law is regularly read out loud so that all listeners can learn about it, that strikes me as compassionate.

WHY, THEN, DID I KEEP hearing friends and classmates refer to Jewish law as "tough" or "harsh"? Did this view come from an actual reading of the text, or was it the result of a centuries-old perception tainted by bias? Part of this disparity in impressions is that the Torah is lived, not just read, and that it is read in conjunction with other texts, but it is also a problem of translation. Some of the language describing Jewish law is misleading, and even incorrect.

Consider the word "commandment" itself. The phrase *aseret hadibrot*, which means "the ten sayings," is what the Ten Commandments are called by the rabbis, the authors of the Talmud—known as *chazal*, an acronym for *chachmeinu zichronam livracha*, or "our sages of blessed memory." This term, *aseret hadibrot*, appears in many rabbinical texts. The singular form of *dibrot* is *diber*, but here, too, there is a popular mistake. Nearly everyone calls a single saying a *dibra*, not a *diber*. The reason for the error is that in Hebrew, most singular masculine nouns are masculine in the plural, but there are exceptions; here, the masculine singular gets a feminine-looking plural. Though the word *dibra* is commonplace, it does not appear in Hebrew dictionaries—because the word *dibra* does not exist.

The Hebrew Bible itself refers to the Ten Commandments simply as *aseret ha'dvarim*—"ten sayings" or "ten statements" or "ten things." This phrase is used in Exodus 34:28 as well as in Deuteronomy 4:13 and 10:4. The Hebrew word *dvarim* means "words" or "things"—not "commandments." The phrase "the Ten Commandments" appears nowhere in the Hebrew.

Paging through various Bibles, I could see how a reader might imagine that the title "The Ten Commandments" appears in the biblical text itself. Though there is no title at all in the Hebrew, some translations, like the 1611 King James Bible, include "The Ten Commandments" as a heading. The Geneva Bible seems to be the first Bible to use the phrase "the tenne commandments," an idea that is then preserved in the King James Version. Tyndale's Bible refers to "the ten verses," which is closer to the Hebrew's "ten sayings." And interestingly, the spot where the King James Bible says the Ten Commandments begin is actually at commandment number two in Jewish tradition.

In Hebrew, the section known as "the Ten Commandments" starts with the words *vayedaber elohim*, "and God said," or "and

God talked." This concept of talking, saying, conversing, is part of how I hear the commandments.

"THE TEN" APPEAR IN THEIR entirety twice in the Hebrew Bible— once in Exodus 20 and once in Deuteronomy 5. There are slight variations between the two versions. Ibn Ezra, the twelfth-century commentator, writes that every word has a body and a soul, and that while these two versions may have different bodies, they have the same soul. One prominent difference is the reason given for keeping the Sabbath; the Exodus version says it is to remember creation, when God worked for six days and rested on the seventh, while the Deuteronomy version says it is to commemorate the exodus from Egypt. Beyond this clear difference, there are differences of opinion between Protestants, Catholics, and Jews on what count as "the ten," and there are further differences between thinkers in each of these traditions.

THE DEBATE ON HOW TO read the ten—and what counts as a *dibra*, or saying—is at least two thousand years old. The first and perhaps most famous point of contention involves whether the words *anochi adonai*, or "I am God," count as one of the ten sayings.

Philo of Alexandria (c. 20 B.C.E.–c. 50 C.E.) saw "I am God" and "Thou shalt not have other gods before me" as one commandment. He considered the two sayings on covetousness as one commandment. The traditional view of *chazal*, or our sages of blessed memory (found in *Mechilta, Yitro, parasha hey*) is that "I am God" is a stand-alone commandment. The traditional Jewish version counts verses 1 and 2 as the first *dibra* and combines verses 3 through 6 as the second. So the sages generally disagree with

Philo on the opening of the ten, but they generally agree that the prohibition against covetousness should be read as one saying.

The words *anochi adonai*, or "I am God," have inspired plenty of fiery commentary over the centuries. Many commentators have noted that it is the only *dibra* that is not written in the imperative. Again and again, the Hebrew commentators zero in on grammar. Then they move on to ways of reading. Nechama Leibowitz (1905–1997), the famous teacher of the Bible, compiled several of these approaches in her book on Exodus, *New Investigations into the Book of Exodus*, published in 1969. Nechama, as she was universally known, traces nearly a thousand years of discussion of the issue of "I am God." She quotes Isaac Abarbanel (1437–1508), a Portuguese Jewish statesman and financier who was also a well-known biblical commentator, who says *anochi*, or "I am," is not a mitzvah—it is not a commandment of belief or action. Instead, Abarbanel says, it is an introduction. It tells the reader who is speaking. Similarly, the Spanish philosopher Rabbi Hasdai ben Judah Crescas (1340–1410) says that anyone who counts "I am God" as one of the positive *mitzvoth*—meaning one of the "thou shalt" commandments—has made a famous error. Crescas says that *mitzvoth*, or deeds—of which there are 613 included in the Torah, both "thou shalts" and "thou shalt nots"—are only things that a person has a choice about; in other words, according to Crescas, "I am God" cannot be a commandment because a person cannot choose to believe.

But then there is the towering figure of the Rambam, Maimonides, who not only believed that "I am God" is a *mitzvah*, a "thou shalt" commandment, but also counted it as a *dibra*, as one of the ten sayings. Maimonides saw the belief in God, and in particular in one God, as the basis of everything.

In his famous volume *Sefer HaMitzvot*, he lists and discusses each of the *mitzvoth*—obligatory deeds as well as prohibited deeds mentioned in the Torah.

The very first deed in his "obligatory deeds" section is belief in God. His sources for it are the two mentions of the *dibrot* in Exodus and Deuteronomy. The first prohibited deed in the "Thou shalt not" section is believing in other gods. For Maimonides, "I am God" and "Thou shalt not have other Gods before me" are the very essence of Judaism.

Ibn Ezra sees the first and second *dibrot* as linked; he understands "I am God" as the subject and "thou shalt not" as the predicate.

Augustine's version, dating from the fifth century, begins with what Judaism traditionally considers the second commandment: "Do not have other gods." To my ear, beginning with a negative— "Thou shalt not have other gods before me"—sounds harsher and more fearsome than the simple, two-word introduction: *anochi adonai,* or "I am God." Perhaps Augustine, who was not always a man of faith and who felt compelled to detail his transgressions in *The Confessions,* one of the earliest surviving autobiographies, was comfortable with the idea of a God who begins with what *not* to do—what *not* to worship.

Martin Luther, in his *Small Catechism,* published in 1529 and intended for the education of children, expresses the First Commandment this way:

Thou shalt have no other gods.

What does this mean?—Answer.

We should fear, love, and trust in God above all things.

The Second Commandment is recorded as:

Thou shalt not take the name of the Lord, thy God, in vain.
What does this mean?—Answer.

We should fear and love God that we may not curse, swear,
use witchcraft, lie, or deceive by His name, but call upon it
in every trouble, pray, praise, and give thanks.

What strikes me most in Luther's version of the First and
Second Commandments is the word "fear." However the commandments are introduced, whether to children or adults, the
introduction matters because it helps the reader imagine the character of God. Consider the possibilities: Is God a God who an-
nounces himself, who simply lays out who He is, for the listener's
understanding, or someone who starts out stern and clear, with
a prohibition against competition—"Thou shalt not have other
gods before me?" It is a choice, too, between beginning with a
positive commandment and a negative one.

When I looked at the heading "The Ten Commandments" in
one of my Bibles, followed by "Thou shalt not have other gods
before me," I began to understand the comment "Mosaic law can
be harsh." But something else gnawed at me. If the word "commandment" is a bit of a stretch, and if "the ten"—the number
and substance—are a matter of debate among faiths and thinkers, then why does the phrase "the Ten Commandments" seem
so solid and indisputable? Though stone or bronze depictions of
the tablets Moses was given are part of the décor of many syna-
gogues, not to mention churches and civic institutions around
the world, the truth is that their layout and arrangement are not a
matter of 100 percent agreement among Jewish rabbis and think-

ers. After all, the Hebrew Bible itself contains two different versions.

The rabbis also have differing ideas on the internal order of the ten. Nachmanides explains that the first five are about the relationship between man and God, while the second five are about the relationship of man to man. Ibn Ezra's reading of the order is more nuanced and complicated. To Ibn Ezra, the division is not the traditional two-part man-God divide, but rather a three-part progression of what makes a human being: heart and mind, speech, and action. The sayings begin with the heart and mind; one must believe in his heart that there is a God. Then they move on to speech—what not to say—and then to action, or how to treat fellow humans. But then in the last five, the order reverses. It is action, then speech, then heart and mind. To Ibn Ezra, then, the order of the *dibrot* has a resonance, and when all are obeyed, they form a portrait of the ideal religious individual, someone whose heart, mind, tongue, and actions all work together.

I was charmed by the way Ibn Ezra writes of his friend, the great medieval poet Rabbi Yehuda HaLevi, coming to him with a question about the *dibrot*. The question of what the sayings and their order meant stumped the great minds of the medieval era—so that one giant had to visit another for insight. Rabbi Yehuda HaLevi's question to Ibn Ezra is: Why does God introduce himself as the God who took you out of Egypt, and not as the God who created the heavens and the earth, and who made you?

This question is about the great themes of the Bible—creation and exodus, birth and freedom, or perhaps birth and rebirth—but it is also about the character of God and the makeup of man. Ibn Ezra's answer is that the degree of belief that people have in their hearts is not equal. For those who truly understand, "I am God" is sufficient. But for those who don't understand, "who took you out of Egypt" is necessary. Those people need an answer to the heretics who approach them about the existence of God. When God performed the miracles in Egypt, everyone saw—the wise and the unwise.

The dialogue between the two great minds is long and often meandering, but what intrigues me most is that both men were interested above all in how the *aseret hadibrot* are presented. Their question is not "Is belief in God a law?" but "Why is God introduced in this way and not another?"

The more I looked at Bibles in translation, the more I, too, became fascinated by presentation. Layout is not simply a matter of punctuation and versification; it also helps frame the understanding of a complicated idea like belief in God, or a law like the prohibition against murder. The Jewish commentators are often very interested in the idea of *smichut*, or what is attached to what; they are therefore interested in which "commandments" are placed next to the murder prohibition. Because many translations alter the Hebrew Bible's versification of the commandments, they also remove this sense of "neighbors in a sentence." By changing the look of the neighborhood of the Ten Commandments, many translations relocate key laws, which affects their tone and perhaps their meaning.

IN HEBREW, FOUR KEY "COMMANDMENTS" are crammed into one verse in Exodus 20:13. But in the 1611 King James Bible, they have more space, with four verses, not one. Each of the four commandments gets star billing, as if each were a lone pole on a prairie of white space:

13 Thou shalt not kill.

14 Thou shalt not commit adultery.

15 Thou shalt not steale.

16 Thou shalt not beare false witnes against thy neighbour.

Reading in my sunroom in an increasingly cold Iowa City, I am shocked by the separation of these powerful statements. But in class, no one around me understands how much of a departure this layout is from the Hebrew. As we read these sections out loud, no one is asking questions about the Ten Commandments, which apparently everyone has seen before, and certainly not about their layout. No one in class questions the relationship between murder, adultery, and theft. Because these three are no longer yoked together in the same verse, it is difficult to imagine why a classmate would even ask such a question. But this is the question that the great medieval commentator Rashi raises. He wants to know what these commandments—crammed into one line in the Hebrew Bible—have in common.

The *dibra* says *lo tirtzach*, "do not murder." There is a difference between "to kill" and "to murder" in Hebrew; the word *laharog* means to kill, whereas *lirtzoach* is to murder. The choice in translation to render "murder" as "kill" in English, as is done in the King James and many other translations that are influenced by it, misstates the legal position of the Hebrew Bible. In various places, the Bible clearly states that in some cases, killing is okay. For instance, if a family member is killed, a relative may kill the killer; if a man comes upon you with the intent to kill you, self-defense is fine. Killing in wartime is sanctioned, and often encouraged. Not so murder.

The next commandment, "Thou shalt not commit adultery," is also only two words: *lo tin'af*. Rashi comments that adultery refers to adultery with a married woman. He quotes Leviticus 20:10, which states that if a married woman commits adultery, she and her lover will both be put to death. "And a man who commits adultery with [another] man's wife, committing adultery with the wife of his fellow the adulterer and the adulteress shall surely be put to death," as the Judaica Press translates.

Rashi, once again, is interested in placement. Why is adultery adjacent to murder? Is all adultery truly on a par with murder? Here, Rashi provides only the answer "adultery with a married woman." It is the reader's task, as always with Rashi, to figure out the question. In this case, the question presumably is, What sort of adultery? Rashi reaches his married-woman conclusion for two reasons: first, he compares it to another place in the Bible, where it is stated that he who sleeps with a married woman will be killed, and second, Rashi is busy scouring for links between murder and adultery, because he, like many Jewish commentators, believes in the *klal*, or reading rule, of *smichut:* that words and ideas that are neighbors are often situated near each other for a reason. Both murder and adultery with a married woman are punishable by death in a Jewish court of law, and it is this fact that connects them in Rashi's mind. The link here is the punishment.

Next, Rashi addresses "Thou shalt not steal." He says that theft here is a theft of souls: kidnapping. Rashi points out that there is a previous prohibition of theft in Leviticus 19:11, so this must refer to a different kind of theft. Then he doubles back and wonders whether perhaps here, in the *aseret hadibrot*, the text refers to stealing money, and Leviticus refers to kidnapping. But he knocks this argument down by saying that we must read in context. He concludes that just as the previous two commandments—prohibiting murder and adultery—specify transgressions that demand capital punishment, so, too, theft here must be a capital offense. This discussion appears in the Talmud in Sanhedrin 86a, and Rashi's thinking follows the same lines.

Interestingly, Rashi does not discuss the fourth of the commandments crammed into the same line: "Thou shalt not bear false witness." But perhaps that is because Deuteronomy 19:16–19 has more to say on it. Here is the 1917 Jewish Publication Society translation of that passage:

> If an unrighteous witness rise up against any man to bear perverted witness against him;
>
> then both the men, between whom the controversy is, shall stand before God, before the priests and the judges that shall be in those days.
>
> And the judges shall inquire diligently; and, behold, if the witness be a false witness, and hath testified falsely against his brother;
>
> then shall ye do unto him, as he had purposed to do unto his brother; so shalt thou put away the evil from the midst of thee.

This passage describes the problem of an *ed zomem*, or a scheming witness. A witness who says that person A did crime A, resulting in punishment B, and who is then found not to have been at the scene of the crime, will get punishment B himself, even if crime A truly was committed by person A—that is how serious false testimony is considered to be. Interestingly, the topic of false witness has obsessed many literary writers; I remember being utterly mesmerized by William Faulkner's "Dry September," a short story about a false accusation of rape. Bernard Malamud's

The Fixer is a novel about a man jailed on false accusations. Jewish law is concerned with preventing such tragedy, and it metes out severe punishment to those who accuse falsely.

However, it is important to understand that there is a difference between law and actual practice. According to Mishna Makkot 1:10, "A Sanhedrin [Jewish high court] that puts a man to death once in seven years is called a murderous one. R. Eleazar ben Azariah says 'Or even once in seventy years.' R. Tarfon and R. Akiva said, 'If we had been in the Sanhedrin no death sentence would ever have been passed.'" So perhaps Jewish law is more talk than harsh punishment. Because there is so much discussion, doubt often ensues.

WHILE THE TEN COMMANDMENTS HAVE engendered much discussion over the centuries, what is not in doubt is the centrality of two plainly stated ideas: the importance of respecting one's parents and the necessity of keeping the Sabbath. In both the Exodus and Deuteronomy versions, those two *dibrot* are neighbors, located smack in the middle of the ten. One commentator even says that the reason for the prominent location of respecting parents is that to honor parents is both a commandment that honors God and one that honors man. Perhaps this is because Shabbat, with its prohibition of work, provides the time—indeed, legislates the time—to talk about the Torah with parents.

Once on Shabbat, when the snow reached all the way to the living room window, I told Abba—my father—that I was learning the *aseret hadibrot*, or the ten sayings, in school. I then proudly discussed the command *lo tachmod*—"Do not covet." I was so pleased that I had noticed the word for cute, *chamud*, hidden inside the word for covet. Finally, I thought, now that I was ten and firmly in the double digits, I was beginning to understand the Bible as my parents did.

"I don't understand that *dibra*," my father said, practically growling. "I never understood it. In fact, I'm not the slightest bit interested in Mrs. L."—and he nodded toward the snow-covered house of an older, padded, rather unglamorous neighbor, also a mother of children and, like all the others, an overworked religious woman in a wig. "Why should I be jealous of anyone? It's ridiculous.

"Frankly," he continued, as I realized I had brought up a topic he must have thought about a lot, "I can't understand why that *dibra* is included."

I AM OFTEN REMINDED OF my father's bafflement at that commandment as I walk through the hot, often jealousy-crazed world of the arts. When I hear friends complain that they have not won a prize, or a contract, or when I read a story of wild jealousy gone violently wrong, I think of my father.

My father simply does not believe in jealousy. He cannot even imagine it, cannot understand the news stories of a wife killing a husband's mistress, or a man cheating in the first place, or any of the varieties of jealous anger. He scoffs at the fire of it, how it burns all the vegetation nearby, how it boils and spills and consumes. And sometimes I think that Shabbat itself, which the sixteenth-century poet Rabbi Shlomo HaLevi Alkabetz called *mekor habracha*—the source of blessing—is the antidote to jealousy, to the temptation to compare and find things less than favorable.

I got to know my father during Shabbat. Perhaps that is why, in the *aseret hadibrot*, honoring our parents and keeping Shabbat are neighbors: because time allows us to know, and honor, our own family. Respecting a person requires time. Moreover, and more deeply, the day in which I got to know my father— Shabbat—allowed me to love what I have. Like my father, I am lucky not to be a victim of jealousy. And so, over years of twenty-five-hour stretches, Shabbat let me see my world and try to approve of it. It let me see Abba, a man few people understand.

Of course I saw him during the week: for dinner, for breakfast, a big tall man with a beard, who ate a lot and sometimes sang. When he got angry, he yelled, rather loudly. He was one of the only fathers who came to all our school plays, who saw me get my very first *siddur*—prayer book—and my very first Chumash— my first Bible. As I stood on the stage to receive them, I saw him seated on the low bench about six inches off the floor with the four-year-olds. He sat there so he could take my picture up close. He had taken half the day off work to see me get a book.

On Sundays he was home, too, but he always had projects: the gutters, the lawn, the washing machine. Sometimes he left papers around the house with numbers and letters scrawled on them. Something plus something, x and y and z and an equal sign. Shabbat was the only time that he was in my sight, not writing and not doing, for all three meals and all the hours in between. I think that in that long expanse, in the Shabbats and all the hours in them, I met him.

Like a parent who ages, who softens, who comes to understand, Shabbat changes with the seasons. It starts with the setting of the sun and ends only after three stars can be seen in the sky the following evening. In the winter, Shabbat is short, energetic, young. The day moves fast. In the summer, like all summer days, it is lazy, long, almost endless. The stars are slow to arrive, showing up around nine P.M. in mid-May, later as the summer yawns on. Shabbat is the one day of the week when I know I will see light become twilight, will watch it happen slowly, second by second, since the workweek cannot begin until the stars arrive.

When I am home, my father and I often take a walk, sometime in the very late afternoon. The great wars of my high school years over mess and disorganization and lateness are over. My father and I have already argued through it all. We have surprised each other, many times.

"I don't know what your system is," my father called to tell me one day, after I had completed a master's degree in poetry in Boston, moved to a new apartment, and found freelance clients. For years he had been upset that I had what he called "no system," that I worked only on what I wanted to work on, and only when I wanted to. "But I have to say, you get a lot done."

That was it, a truce. A compliment.

We were finally not just father and daughter, but friends.

THE BIBLE'S *DIBRA* ABOUT PARENTS has a strange word choice. We are not commanded to love our parents, or even to like them. The Hebrew is *kabed et aveecha ve'et eemacha*. The word *kabed* is an imperative verb, and it is related to the noun *kaved*, or heavy. There should be some heft to the way we feel about our parents.

"Treat your father and mother with heft." The verb *kabed* is frequently translated as "honor," an accurate translation, and maybe honor has a heft to it. But the root, *kbd*, should not be ignored. The idea is to treat your parents with heavy consideration, to make sure they have a serious place in your life.

The commandment regarding the Sabbath is similar. It is not to love the Sabbath, or even to like it, but to keep it. What Shabbat is about is a commandment to respect time—to let time also have a prime place in your life.

When I walk with my father on Shabbat, I think of both these things. On trips home from Iowa during school breaks, my father and I often take Shabbat walks. We leave the house together in the hot sun and return in the blue grayness of the in-between. On my last visit home, for instance, we walked down our block, once all old pear trees and single-family homes, now two- and three- and four-family dwellings, the yards bursting with children, the trees sometimes removed to make room. Building codes give way when votes and offices are at stake, and real estate prices make everyone a little crazy, a little woozy, a little more willing to overlook the conversion of a garage into an apartment. By now, almost everyone has an apartment in their former garage. My father, always the mathematician, noted the increasing number of garbage bags.

"I would not like to be a garbage man on this block," he said.

I laughed. It's an old joke. This block would be the worst block in the world to be a garbageman. After Shabbat, after the holidays, and worse—this year, after Shabbat plus the holidays' three-day fest, the number of bags will be staggering.

And yet I know my father is happy when he takes out a lot of garbage. When the other kids are home and I am in Iowa, he calls to tell me how much orange juice he bought, how much milk, how many garbage bags he had to set out, instead of the one he now sets out because only he and my mother are in the house.

We are still staring at the large number of garbage bags when two Chassidic women, in stockings with seams up the back, their hair in shining wigs and their necks graced by modest pearls, pass by. They look away from my father.

"*Gut Shabbos,*" I say, in Yiddish.

Neither woman answers. Women won't speak to my father, because he is a man. They sometimes don't answer me for other reasons: because they can't figure out why I'm dressed so casually, sneakers and a skirt, or because I'm not Chassidic, not exactly one of them.

A few seconds later, some young men pass by. They quickly look away from me, focusing on the trees across the street. I am used to this. Men around here won't look me in the eye, won't look at me at all. They'll put up a curtain down the middle of a bus to avoid catching a glimpse of me. If the curtain falls, the casualty of a bus suddenly stopping short, they rush to put it back up.

My father is trying to explain how happy he is with his latest paper, "Allocation Rules for Adaptive Repeated Measurements Designs." I nod. I like the sound of his specialty—*optimal experimental design*—even if I can't follow the detailed theories, the dreamy calculations of pure math and statistics, the hope of creating the best possible experiment. His previous paper was also about optimal experiments and efficiency, two universes that I do not walk in.

We walk downhill, past a house that has been converted into a synagogue. And past another house that has been converted into a synagogue. Make your house into a shul or a *beit midrash*, a place of learning, and you won't pay taxes. It's a popular choice, unless you are the neighbor dealing with the traffic and the parking problems and the noise, and never the beneficiary of the government's largesse. Sometimes the house is gone entirely, and in the space where once there was a modest four-bedroom house there is now an immense, towering synagogue. That's what there is now, on Francis, the next street.

My father reads me the Yiddish inscription on the walls of the building. We both notice that there are new signs: parking

signs, and signs that say PLEASE DON'T BLOCK THE MAILBOX AFTER
TEN A.M. We are both pleased by these small signs, some attempt,
finally, at politeness, some concern for others.

The next street is Ronald Drive, where the houses have
curved roofs meant to mimic the roofs of houses in China. There
are new sidewalks, because of all the people who walk on Shabbat.
The sidewalks are packed; the crowds make it feel like a miniature
Manhattan. Most people say *"Gut Shabbos"* to one another, but no
one talks to us.

Only in a town as committed to exclusion as our town—
exclusion from the rest of the world, and from the rest of the
Jewish world—could a person as friendly as my father have so few
friends. He talks to supermarket cashiers. He has what he calls
"pleasant and informative" conversations with the Internal Reve-
nue Service. And I—a person approached constantly by strangers,
whose job it is to interview, to make others comfortable—only
here, in this town, does no one ever speak with me.

Maybe because we lived here, isolated among the crowds,
among all the little Chassidic sects and all the individual rabbis,
we learned to know one another. Only after leaving home and living in many faraway places do I understand what my mother said
about her father—my grandfather Saba Shmuel.

"I always knew he was my friend," she said.

There is also what my father said about meeting that same
man, my mother's father, for the first time. "He had so much respect for his daughter," Abba said, "I just couldn't believe it. I had
never seen a father like that."

PERHAPS A RELATED THOUGH UNWRITTEN aspect of the command
to honor parents is an implied message about how to treat chil-

dren. How is a child supposed to know how to honor? The Bible does not offer details, but maybe it is the parent's job to model respect. I got to see what my father did not see as a boy: respect the other way, father to child. And like my mother, who grew up with an unusual man as a father, I am honored to have a man like my father as my friend. Maybe that is the deeper side of the command to honor your father and your mother, to me the most mysterious of the Ten Commandments.

My father and I walk slowly down the hill, toward Suzanne Lake. The sidewalks are so full of people that hundreds of them are walking in the street, where, of course, there are no cars on Shabbat. I notice the old metal sign: KEEP OUR COMMUNITY CLEAN. It is meant to discourage throwing diapers and potato chip bags into the lake, but I know that if they could, some of the neighbors would clean us out, too. We, too, would be floating in the lake.

"What are you doing here?" neighbors say to my parents. I know, watching the crowds watch us, that everyone around us is wondering that again. The neighbors are not shy about their wishes for us. Once, my parents got a flurry of phone calls. Someone had taken out an ad in a local Yiddish newspaper that said "The Kushners"—it listed our address—"are selling their house." My parents weren't selling. As for who placed the ad, we still don't know, and I am 100 percent certain that my father does not care. Gossip is as incomprehensible to him as jealousy.

With the snafu over the ad, my father taught me what he has always taught me: how to ignore the disapproval of the world, no matter how loud it is. He taught me how to listen to myself, and how to hear that same thing in other people and places: the quiet beating of the individual heart.

* * *

AT SUZANNE LAKE, WHICH HAS been part of my life for so long that it feels like an extension of my body, my father and I check on the progress of the white duck. There are lots of gray ducks, and black-feathered ducks, but only one white one. My father is excessively concerned with the white duck's social life.

"I wonder if he has made a friend," he says.

Usually we come here to watch the white duck swimming alone. The other ducks group together: dozens of them. Sometimes my father waves his arms at the white duck, and I have even heard him talk to the duck, in what he believes are duck sounds. The duck, to my surprise, always seems calm and pleased to be spoken to by a human.

This time, the white duck is not there.

My father is horribly disappointed. I am sad that this particular Shabbat walk to the lake has not turned out well. The walk to the lake, familiar as it is, is the major kind of traveling I have done with my father, the major kind of traveling he does, period. Abba's sudden trip to Israel—the year after the Six-Day War—is the only story I have ever heard of his actually volunteering to travel. Unlike my mother, who will go anywhere, just as she will learn any language, from any ancient land, my father has definite boundaries, things he will not do. Today, he drives across the country to visit his children instead of taking a plane; he regularly declines invitations to speak at conferences if they are even an hour or so away. When he flew to Israel, he avoided stopovers in Europe. He will not, he says, accidentally support a soda merchant who once had a hand in genocide. The last thing he wants is to have to buy a soda in the airport.

My father likes to say he is not like me, his daughter who wrote a travel column during wartime in Israel, who will go anywhere for a story. He is not like his other daughter, my sister, who for years jetted around the country for consulting jobs. But I suppose my father's borders—where he will go, and especially where he will absolutely not go—are rooted in hope, a higher standard, a certain kind of belief.

For thirty years he has worked as a research scientist at an institute twenty minutes from home. Five days a week, my father comes up with advanced mathematical solutions—mathematical dreams, or maybe mathematical utopias—for the experiments of the future. He comes up with concepts like the Kushner Theorem, the subject of part of a course at the University of Illinois, which a French scientist recently referred to as the Theorème de Kushner. It was because of his love of theorems that we ended up in this town. Because jobs that require mathematical skills are hard to find, and my father wanted one. Because Monsey was the closest Jewish community, the kind of place with a school in which we could learn to read the Bible. Because my father, from the beginning, stood for doing what you love, even if the money is not great and the circumstances not perfect. So for many years, my parents raised five kids on one salary—a government scientist's salary. And so my father showed us what I believe he believes: work is the reward of work, just as rest is the reward of rest.

THESE ARE THE THINGS THAT are rewarded in this world, the rabbis teach in *Pirkei Avot*, or *Ethics of the Fathers*, and these are the things for which a person gets the principal in this world. But the interest comes in the next world.

I sometimes wish that I believed without a doubt in the idea and ultimate power of God, the way so many of the people I have known believed. If I believed in that way, I would most likely believe in reward. I would most likely believe in a next world. In-

stead, I think the reward of living a just life is a just life. The
reward of a father, I suppose, is to be a father. The reward of a
daughter, I know, is to be a daughter.

The reward of reading is the experience of reading. And perhaps the reward of keeping the laws is just that, even though vio-
lation of those laws is not punishable in a clear way by a sitting
court, the way, say, theft in New York City is clearly punishable
by a local judge. Instead, Judaism expects a person to repent, to
change on the inside, to develop an internal sense of justice. This
is the opposite of the harshness some readers hear in the Bible; it
is a call for personal responsibility. What Jewish law asks for can
be heard in the verb *vayedaber,* "and he talked," the verb that opens
the *aseret hadibrot,* the ten sayings that are translated as the Ten
Commandments. It can be heard in the simple introduction—*Ani
adonai,* I am God, which perhaps requires the listener to wonder
who he is or who she is. How would I introduce myself to God,
if I had to?

What Jewish law wants is an ongoing conversation between
man and God, and between man and man—but most of all, between man and himself. It's not a command, exactly, but a conversation: an inner song, full of melody and refrain, sometimes heard
only by what Rabbi Soloveitchik so movingly called the lonely
man of faith.

SONG

———◆———

תרגום

דְּאָתֵי יִתְרוֹן צַדִּיקַיָּא
אָמֵן וְאָמֵן: א לְשַׁבְּחָא
בְּשֻׁבְחָא טָבָא עַל יְדֵיהוֹן
דִּבְנֵי קֹרַח: ב הֵיךְ אַיָּלָא
דִּי תְּרַע עַל פְּצִידֵי מַיָּא
הֵיכְנָא נַפְשִׁי תִּרְגָּא
לוֹתָךְ יְיָ: ג צָחַת לָךְ

ת״א כל פימור מז טקדיה ספר קן
כאול מפדום. מכר ויקל
אתרי פות ופנתם

מנחת שי
מב (ב) אפיקי מים. ל:כ״ב

יְהֹוָה ׀ אֱלֹהֵי יִשְׂרָאֵל מֵהָעוֹלָם וְעַד
הָעוֹלָם אָמֵן ׀ וְאָמֵן:

ס פ ר שׁ ני

מב א לַמְנַצֵּחַ מַשְׂכִּיל לִבְנֵי־קֹרַח:
ב כְּאַיָּל תַּעֲרֹג עַל־אֲפִיקֵי־מָיִם
כֵּן נַפְשִׁי תַעֲרֹג אֵלֶיךָ אֱלֹהִים: ג צָמְאָה

רש״י

מב (א) לבני קרח. אסיר ואלקנה ואביאסף הם היו
החלה בעצה אביהם ובשעת המחלוקת פרשו
וכשנכלעו. כל סביבותם ופתהה הארץ פיה נשאר מקום'
לתוך פי הארץ כענין שנאמר ובני קרח לא מתו ושם אמרו
שירה ושם יסדו המזמורים האלו ועלו משם ושרת' עליהם
רה״ו ונתנבאו על גלויו' הבי' ועל חורבן בית' ועל מלכות בית
דוד : (ב) כאיל תערוג על אפיקי. א' ערב נטפל על
קול האיל כאשר יפול ל' נהם ושקוק לדוד ונעה
לשוורים ובפצות לעומתית אמרו רד״ל האילה הזאת הסירה
שבחיות וכשהכיר' לחמתה למים הם מחכנסות אליה שתחלה
עיניה וגועה והקב״ה מרחם עליה והההום מעלה לה מים'
לתוֹך הערוג. כאילת תערוג לא נאמר וכל'י ירעוג לא
נאמר אלא כאיל כאיל תערוג דבר הכ'.בזכר ונקיבה לא הזכר
קול עמק תערוג כמו שפירשנו נטפת ברמה שלה ורמהות נטפת. ומנגם הבר תערוג

אבן עזרא

והפך עלי למשחית ולפי דעתי די פיוט תחלתו משכיל:
מב (א) כאיל. ידוע הוא דבר כאיל האיל הנכספים שתתחמם
קרבו או בקש אפיקי מים חזקים ואיל על גאל נקבה כמו עז
בת שנה: (ג) צמאה. הט'' ירוו האדם רע ויחיה ותשוב
נפשי אליו ולא לו הלמם ע'כ למה הכסם לבית השם כהכסף

מצודת דוד

(יד) ברוך ה'. נתן הודאה לגאל מבלתו הספר על אשר נתן טו רום
ה' לגמד ט': מהעולם. ל'ם מקום העולם עד קלהו: אמן
ואמן. הוא מדך הטוב אשר אחר הברכה נהיה מקום:
מב (א) משכיל. הם למדו דעת והשכל לההפלל על הגלות: (ב) בליוות
הלמבת כן נפשי וגו': (ג) צמאה נפשי. מתאוה אני למם אלהים כמו

מצודת ציון

מב (ב) תערג. כן נקרא' שאגת האיל וכמו נהם לארי ושוקק
לדוד והדומים: אפיקי. הם המקומות הגרים ישם המים

באור המלות — מלבי״ם

מב (ב) כאיל. איל שם כולל זכרים ונקבות, והנקבה
ערוגת ביותר מהזכר, ותערג, תהמה,
כמו גניה לשור. והגה לינה, ונביחה לכלב, ושאגה
ונהימה לאריות, וכדומה:

תפלות דוד — באור הענין

קרח, ונגד הברכות וההתהלות שברך והלל עד עתה
בספר הזה, אמר שברכות אלו יהיו בפי ישראל מן
העולם ועד העולם לדור דורים, אמן ואמן:

מב (א) למנצח משכיל לבני קרח, מזמור זה הוסד
מאת המנצחים מבני קרח, על

גלות, ונחלק לשלושה חלקים, כי בגלותינו נעדרו ממנו שני ענינים נכבדים שהיה לנו בימי קדם, א] גילוי
שכינה והנבואה, ב] האותות והמופתים, כמ"ש אותותינו לא ראינו אין עוד נביא, כי בשני אלה נכבדנו בימי
קדם, כמ"ש השמע עם קול אלהים חיים או הנסה אלהים לבא לקחת לו גוי מקרב גוי במסות באותות
ובמופתים, ואמר (ישעיה ס"ג) איה המעלם מים את רועה צאנו איה השם בקרבו את רוח קדשו, חאת
שלישית הגלות בעצמו שהוא הפירוד שהיו מפוזרים אז בין עכו"ם סובלים צער ומכאובות, והם אלהים
ענינים מיוחדים, אן העדר הנבואה ורוה"ק וגילוי שכינה, הוא ענין הנוגע להנפש אשר היא בת אלהים
ומשתוקקת אל הדבור הזה הנפלא שחסר לה עתה, וע"ז הוסד החלק הראשון, טענת הנפש ע"ז ותנחומותי

רד״ק

הָעוֹלָם. מהזמן הראשון עד זמן האחרון כל הימים
קיום. וקיום. כמו שעונו אדם מנו אחר הברכה לקיים הברכה
כי אמן לשון קיום: (א) למנצח. יתכן לפרש כי דוד חבר אלה
העמוקים כרוח הקדש ונתנם לבני קרח המשוררים הנמצאים
בזמנו. ולפי שבני קרח היו נביאים יהם אלה כן בני בניהם אליהם
ונאר לפני בניהם לקצר. וזה. המזמור יש אומרים כי אמרו
בראשונה גולה. בין פלשתים ויש אומרים כי נאמר על לשון בני
הגלות ואסרו בלי יחיד ונאמר על אחד מבני הגלות
דומה וצוקם מן הגלות שיתאוה לארץ הקדש לשוב הכבוד
עליה. וזהו אליך אלהים: (ג) כאיל. יש אומרים כי במדבר
בטקום שאין מים מציים יתאוו לפים ועוד כי יאכל האיל נחשים
ויתהמם וילכן חיים להתקרר ווהו מעם אפיק מים שהם
פים הגרים שם. גם יש אומרים כי האילים כשרודפים
אחריהם הכלבים הצדים לבן אחריהם. אזו שמצאו פים
עמוקים הולכים וחורגים ויכאו בתוך המם עיפים וינצלו מהם
ואמר איל לשון זכר ותערוג לשון נקבה כולל זכרים ונקבות.
או אמר תערוג כי אפשר לי האילה שהערוג יותר מן הזכר כי
תערוג והגאלף סרוב תאוה וגילן כריגה נוגל על האיל כמו
לשון גניה בשר. לא אמר רעבה כי יהיה האדם.
גילל ורהמה נר והוא טועקת והקב״ה מרחם ומזמן להם הצמא

כְּאַיָּל
K'ayal
Like a deer

תַּעֲרֹג
ta'arog
will crave/yearn [written in future tense but should be understood as a general statement in present tense, namely "craves" or "yearns"]

עַל־
al
at

אֲפִיקֵי־
afikei
the riverbank of [plural in Hebrew]

מָיִם
mayim
water

כֵּן
ken
so

נַפְשִׁי
nafshi
my soul

תַּעֲרֹג
ta'arog
will crave/yearn

אֵלֶיךָ
eleicha
to/for you

אֱלֹהִים
elohim
God

צָמְאָה
tzam'ah
thirsts

נַפְשִׁי
nafshi
my soul

לֵאלֹהִים
ley'lohim
to/for God

לְאֵל
l'el
to God

חָי
chai
living/alive

[Phrase *l'el chai* = for/to the living God]

מָתַי	אָבוֹא	וְאֵרָאֶה
matai	*avoh*	*v'erah'eh*
when	will I come	and will I be seen

פְּנֵי	אֱלֹהִים
p'nei	*elohim*
the face of; before	God

As the deer panteth for the water
So my soul longeth after you

> Martin J. Nystrom (based on Psalm 42,
> a well-known praise song, 1981)

1 As a deer longs for flowing streams,
so my soul longs for you, O God.

> New Oxford Annotated Bible: New Revised
> Standard Version with the Apocrypha (2010)

1 [To the chiefe Musician, Maschil, for the sonnes of Korah.] As
the Hart panteth after the water brookes, so panteth my soule
after thee, O God.

> King James Bible (1611)

To the choirmaster. A Maskil of the Sons of Korah.

42 As a deer pants for flowing
streams,
so pants my soul for you, O God.

> English Standard Version (Crossway Bibles, 2011)

THE TEN-YEAR-OLD BOY CRIED THE FORTY-SECOND PSALM SO loudly that my feet shook on the bench I was standing on. "Will you stop that?" the girl next to me said. I tried hard to remain still. That's what I was there for: to be seen and not to say what I thought. We were practicing for our graduation from the eighth grade. In September, I would be in Manhattan, in a school where boys and girls shared classrooms and a curriculum. That was not true at the school I was graduating from, where boys were taught Talmud for hours every morning while girls were not. In the yeshiva world, Talmud is far more prestigious than Torah. Talmud is the gold standard, the "real thing," and it took a lot of hours. Boys were in their own classrooms all day, except for forty-five minutes of math and another forty-five minutes of science, which for some reason were about ability and not gender. I was completing my ninth year at the school, where I was in class six days a week with the same group of twenty-four girls I'd been with since kindergarten. I would never spend so many hours of my life with the same group of classmates again. I would never again know how every one of my classmates behaved in every subject, what their parents and grandparents and siblings were like, what kind of houses they lived in and what food they ate. Never again would a school that put girls and boys in separate classrooms seem "modern" to me just because every other school in town had girls and boys in separate buildings, or separate neighborhoods.

The boy singing was the younger brother of one of my classmates. He had a solo, and every other word out of his mouth was *oy*. Of course no girl was allowed to have a solo, since none of us were allowed to sing alone in public; the school observed the prohibition against *kol isha*, the voice of a woman—women could not be heard singing because a woman's voice was considered the voice of temptation. I wondered whether he'd gotten the solo because his family was wealthy, or because his voice had not changed yet, or simply because someone thought he had a pleasant voice. The family was in the sweater business, if I remember correctly. His voice was pure longing, and even though I never saw him again after I graduated—I never saw most of the boys ever again, because they went to boys' high school and then boys' seminary, and by then I was gone—his voice is the voice in which I will always hear the psalm, the hopeless song of a boy who would really love to grow up. Standing on that bench and trying not to move, I heard:

Ke'ayohl ta'aroyg al afikei moyim, ken nafshi ta'aroyg, eleicha eloykim.
As the deer craves the riverbank, so my soul craves you, God.

Wherever the vowel *o* appeared in the Hebrew, the boy turned it into an *oy*. Wherever the name of God was mentioned— *elohim*—he transformed it in two ways. First, he replaced the *h* with a *k*, which is what religious Jews do when they are not actually praying and need to speak the name of God; they alter it, make it less holy, so as not to desecrate it, just as I did on my classmate's page in Iowa. But instead of saying *elokim*, he sang *eloykim*, changing the *o* to *oy*. Adding the *oy* made the word sound the way the Chassidim pronounce it; something about that *oy* sounded more religious and soulful, which was probably what he wanted—it was regarded as a good thing, back then, to seem

more devout than one was. The recorded music that plays in the
kosher stores of Monsey often has plenty of *oys* in it, even when
it reproduces biblical phrases in which there is no *oy* at all. Or
maybe the boy was just imitating the way his grandfather said it,
echoing the old pronunciation of a European Jewish community
that was mostly burned to the ground. As for *ta'arog*, which comes
from the word *erga*—deep desire—he made it into *ta'aroyg*, getting an *oy* in there too. He was chubby and black-haired, with
light eyes, and he could sing and cry like a little girl. He was there
to cry for the boys and the girls, and he was good at it. After he
sang the first lines, eyes shut, microphone close to his lips, he suddenly broke into the high part of the song. Here the *oys* reached
new crescendos. "*Oy tzama oya nafshi l'eyloykim.*" Literally: "My
soul thirsts for God." The boy's high cry and the flurry of *oys*
evoked a sense of hopelessness. When would he ever see a living
God? Never, and he seemed to know it. He was singing about a
constant craving. He sang like he was singing for God personally,
and even though I tried not to move my feet, by the time he got
to the part about seeing the face of God—*matai avoh v'eraeh p'nei
elohim*, or "When shall I come and behold the face of God?" as
the Oxford translates it—the bench beneath my feet was shaking
again.

All the songs from my elementary school graduation were
about a craving for God, a deep desire for a life of faith. At the
time I knew nothing but the life of faith, so I don't think I was
able to imagine the craving for it. As for craving water, that was
impossible to imagine also. We were minutes away from the ma-
jestic Hudson, and high school, the glittering freedom of Manhattan, lay just over that water. Four years later, my high school
graduation featured the same Psalm 42, set to music. The melody
was completely different, as were the circumstances. "Deer" was

pronounced according to the modern Hebrew, with an Israeli accent—*ke'ayal*. There were none of the *oys* of my childhood, of my small, deeply religious hometown. Here the girls sang alone, as well as along with the boys.

As a deer craves the riverbank, so I crave you, oh God.

Driving through Iowa, I sometimes sing both melodies to myself in the car. And though the second is the more sophisticated, with a part that was tailor-made for my voice, I like the first better, *oys* and all. When I want to remember home, that's the psalm I sing. And I turn one line over in my mind: "My soul thirsts for God."

That line is starting to make more sense as I read through a stack of translations. I am thinking about the idea of thirsting for divinity more than I ever thought I would. So many of the Psalms are about desire. They are about the glory of God, what Gerard Manley Hopkins called "God's grandeur," and about the human inability to approach it. They are about beauty and thirst. Water and craving. When I opened the 1611 King James Version, I heard the thirst in the first two verses of the psalm:

As the Hart panteth after the water brookes, so panteth my soule after thee, O God.
My soule thirsteth for God, for the liuing God: when shall I come and appeare before God?

The King James version of this psalm opens with a panting, instead of the Hebrew's simply stated *ta'arog*, or craving. Throughout the King James Version, everything sounds louder. It changes a silent craving into a huff:

As the Hart **panteth** after the water brookes, so **panteth**
my soule after thee, O God.

Reading the King James Version, I immediately missed a key
feature of the Hebrew. In Hebrew, *mayim* is the word for water
and *elohim* is the name of God used in the first two verses. *Mayim*
and *elohim* rhyme; water and God are therefore paired in Hebrew.
It is part of the poignancy of the psalm, this rhyme of the visible
and the invisible, the knowable and the unknowable. It is part of
what makes this psalm easy to memorize and sing, and difficult to
forget. Man can see water but can never see God. In verse 3, the
Hebrew name for God, *elohim*, appears twice:

> *Tzamah nafshi l'****elohim l'el chai*** *matai avoh v'eraeh p'nei*
> ***elohim***.

A literal translation might read:

> My soul thirsts for God, for the living God. When will I
> come and be seen by the face of God?

But then, beginning in verse 3, how God is referred to starts
to change. The first mention of God, *elohim*, is the same word that
appears in Genesis 1:1—the word for God that is both plural in
form and singular in meaning. But the second mention is *el chai*,
the living God. God is further defined as a present God, a God
who is there. And in the fourth verse, God is *eloheicha*—your God
(singular "your," as in a god belonging to one person). This "your
God" has a mocking tone to it; the implication is that maybe your
God, this so-called *el chai*, this living God, is not there after all. If
your God is not there, then where is he? Verse 4 reads:

*Hayta li deemati lechem yomam va'layla b'emor elai kol hayom
ayeh eloheicha.*

In the 1917 Jewish Publication Society translation, it reads:

My tears have been my food day and night, while they say
unto me all the day: "Where is thy God?"

In verse 5, *elohim* returns, as part of a memory; the speaker
remembers how he went with the crowd to *beit elohim*, the house
of God. "These things I remember, and pour out my soul within
me, / how I passed on with the throng, and led them to the house
of God, / with the voice of joy and praise, a multitude keeping
holyday," the 1917 Jewish Publication Society translation continues. And in verse 6, the soul tells itself to praise *elohim*, to praise
God. But in verse 7, the psalm turns intimate and personal. Now
it is no longer about *elohim*, or *eloheicha*, but *elohai*—my God. The
intimacy continues to increase. By verse 9, the psalm describes
how at night, *shiro imi*—His song is with me. The speaker is saying a prayer to *el chayai*—the God of my life. The back-and-forth
that occurs earlier in the psalm returns in verse 11, with adversar-
ies who say, all day, *ayeh eloheicha?*—"Where is your God?" The
word *ayeh* is the same word God uses when he asks Cain where his
brother is. Here in verse 11, the taunts about the absence of God
rise again. Verse 12 includes the heartbreaking conversation with
the psalmist's own soul, but it ends with the praise of *elohai*—"my
God."

The psalms are songs, and in English I miss the musical elements of this verse that do not cross over from the Hebrew. In the
movement from one language to another, the music necessarily
changes. But here, the echoing of other places in the Bible, and

especially a well-known passage about the need to study the Bible continually, are no longer accessible to an English reader. In the Hebrew, the transliterated version of verse 4 reads:

Hayta deem'ah'tee lechem yomam va'layla beh'ehmor eylai kol hayom ayeh eloheicha.

Note the alliteration of the letters *m* and *l* in this line, which does not come through in translation:

My tears have been my food day and night; I am ever
taunted with, "Where is your God?"
> Jewish Publication Society Bible (1985)

The words *yomam va'layla* are translated as "day and night." And yet it's not the common "day and night," which would be *yom va'layla*; in Hebrew, *yom* is day and *layla* is night. The breathing is different in the two versions: *yom va'layla* generally requires a breath between *yom* and *va'layla*. But *yomam* is different, with its accent on the second syllable, and it allows the speaker to say both words together, without stopping, emphasizing the sense of something continual, day blending into night.

The reader of Hebrew who knows the Bible well will recognize the somewhat unusual expression *yomam va'layla* from Joshua 1:8, Isaiah 34:10, and Jeremiah 33:20. The most famous use of this expression is the one that appears in Joshua 1:8, where the people of Israel are exhorted to stick to the Torah, to study it *yomam va'layla*—continuously, without stopping.

In Psalm 42, the same expression used to indicate the need to study day and night is now used to indicate how, day and night, the speaker is eating his own tears; later, in the second part of that verse, the speaker is asked where his God is. It is as if the entire way of life of the Torah is being questioned, suggesting that "your way of life is not one of continual study, but continual tears." And just after that, in the second half of verse 4, we hear others asking all day, "Where is thy God?" What is critical is that *others* are asking this question.

THE QUESTION "WHEN WILL I see God"—as opposed to "Where is thy God?" or "When will your God show up?"—is one that appears in various forms throughout the Bible. In the beginning, the Bible presents God as the asker of questions. In the Garden of Eden, God asks Adam, "Where are you?" God asks Cain a version of the same question—"Where is your brother?" And then, as the Bible continues, the situation flips. Man asks God questions. Job confronts God; Isaiah has some tough questions for God. So does Jeremiah. As we graduates left school and walked into the world, we were no longer the children answering questions about God in classrooms. Instead, like so many who walked before us, we, too, found ourselves asking God where he was.

This progression is exactly what the psalm describes. In verse 3, the soul is thirsting for God, hoping to come before God. In the 1917 Jewish Publication Society translation, it reads: "My soul thirsteth for God, for the living God: When shall I come and appear before God?" But by verse 4, the difficulties of life have seeped in. "My tears have been my food day and night [*yomam va'layla*], while they say unto me all the day: 'Where is thy God?'" The King James Version expresses the sense of continuity implied in *yomam va'layla* with "I continually say," and yet this conveys more of a feeling of repetition than an ongoing action. The Jewish Publication Society translation of 1985 highlights the "while they

say unto me" by phrasing it as "I have been taunted." This is an interesting choice; the Hebrew is simply "said to me"—*b'emor elai*—
but the fact that the saying does not stop makes it a taunt. As a
child, I did not understand this mocking question "Where is your
God?" Years later, after a car burst to bits in front of my apartment
in Jerusalem, after immense buildings in lower Manhattan were
burned to the ground by airplane fuel and anger, I understand it
better. The ugliness of life directly confronts the speaker's original faith in God and craving for God. Verse 4 comes right after
verse 3, but the question of verse 3—"When will I be able to see
God?"—already seems far away. By verse 4, that question has been
flipped into a source of mockery—"Where is your God?"

It is moving and notable that the Psalmist himself does not ask
God, "Where are you, my God?" In verse 5, instead of attempting
to answer the question "Where is your God?"—a question that
is of course impossible to answer—the psalm turns inward. This
is the most interesting and unforgettable part of Psalm 42: not
what it tells others but rather how well it captures what we tell
ourselves.

Beginning with verse 5, and the clause "when I think of
these things," the psalm goes on to describe the most private of
moments—a silent conversation with oneself. "This Psalm is re-
markable for the inner dialogue it relates," the note in the Jewish Study Bible says, articulating what I have always felt, in New
York, in Jerusalem, in Iowa. The psalm itself, as it continues, is
about thinking about the psalm. It mimics the experience of a
devout person getting older, of a reader looking out at the world
and seeing that yes, indeed, terrible things happen to wonderful people, while so many holy texts continue to insist that God
exists and that good will come to those who believe. The psalm
records the speaker's incredibly honest reaction to this all-too-

familiar reality. The speaker in verse 5, in the Jewish Publication Society translation—first published in 1973 and revised in
1997—remembers how fervently he once believed, how all around
him were the joyous sounds of praise:

> When I think of this, I pour out my soul:
> How I walked with the crowd,
> Moved with them, the festive throng, to the House of God
> With joyous shouts of praise.

That's the boy I remember, singing at the top of his lungs at graduation; and then life happens. And incredibly, in the very next
verse, verse 6, the Psalmist admits that he and his soul are duking
it out. He owns up to the sadness:

> Why so downcast, my soul,
> Why disquieted within me?

And yet, the answer to "Why so downcast, my soul" is obvious. The soul wants to see God, but God cannot be seen. This
is an astonishing moment of honesty, of admitting the limits of
faith right in the middle of a poem of praise of God. It is the
story not only of the search for God, but of many great hopes
and many overwhelming desires that feel like a thirst for water.
But then, as soon as the Psalmist admits the limits of his faith,
the psalm twists again. In the next two lines, it returns to faith, to
the believer's idea of praise despite it all. I think of W. H. Auden's
"In Memory of W. B. Yeats," written on the eve of World War II,
which ends with the unforgettable lines "In the prison of his
days / Teach the free man how to praise." This impulse or need
to insist on praise in a time of disaster appears movingly here, at

the end of the psalm, which veers back to praise just in time to close the book on the shocking moment of doubt that has just been revealed:

Have hope in God;
I will yet praise Him
For His saving presence.

That's familiar stuff at the end, but it doesn't erase all the twists in the middle. These twists of faith are part of the reason I keep returning to this psalm, which reflects my own changes in thought, perhaps the changes all of us experience in how we view God. The psalm is, above all, "a dialogue of self and soul," not unlike Yeats's famous poem of that name. The psalm is there for me whenever I am trying to understand the world within me. It also seems to arrive whenever I am attempting to understand the world without.

When I went to church for the first time, with a friend who is the son of a minister, Psalm 42 happened to be projected in yellow letters on a huge video screen with a purple background. The pianist was also a friend of mine, the reason we had come, and she was accompanied by a man on the electric guitar and a small choir of both men and women.

As a deer longs for water . . .

That's what the screen said, in the version of the psalm used in that particular Methodist church, only a few minutes' drive from my house in Iowa City. The melody was cheerful, not an ounce of desperation in it. I thought of the slow, mournful rendition I had been taught in high school. And I noticed something. In the Hebrew psalm, the word *afikei* comes before the word for water, modifying it. *Afikei* means "riverbank," the border of the water, the edge of it. In the church version, that little extra word had been eliminated. And yet it's not the water the deer longs for, but the *edge* of the water. The word *afikei* is an ancient Hebrew word, related to the Ugaritic *afk* and the Syriac *afka*. Translators into English have struggled with it, and with the phrase *afikei mayim*—the word *mayim* means "water"—trying everything from "the water brooks" in the 1945 Soncino edition to Robert Alter's "streams of water" in 2007 to the rather startling "fountains" in the 1750 Challoner revision of the Douay-Rheims. But "water" alone doesn't catch the meaning here. Throughout the psalm, language is modified; it is in the language of "almost," in the tongue of simile: you can *almost* have it, *almost* taste it. It is not a deer, but "like a deer," a slight distance conveyed by the single letter *k'* in Hebrew, which sometimes disappears in translation. And it matters that what is described is not simply the water but the riverbank, the edge of the water, the border between water and land. It matters that what happens later in the psalm is *almost* an expression of complete doubt, and *almost* an expression of complete faith. The language of the psalm is about borders, and at every turn it mirrors the distance between the Psalmist and what he most wants.

THE TRANSLATIONS OF PSALM 42 struggle to convey the degrees of craving. They ratchet it up or down, and occasionally they overdo it. The Jewish Publication Society adds several O's where none exist in Hebrew:

Like a hind crying for water
my soul cries for You, O God;
my soul thirsts for God, the living God;
O when will I come to appear before God!

The 1750 Challoner revision of the 1610 Douay-Rheims Bible adds adjectives to the Hebrew, and it even includes two explanatory phrases at the top that attempt to put the psalm in context. In the Challoner revision, God is described as "the strong living God," but "strong" does not appear in the Hebrew. In verse 4, there is a "wonderful tabernacle," but "wonderful" is not in the Hebrew either. The Challoner revision also has "fountains" of water, which is certainly not what is going on in the Hebrew psalm. Taken together, these decisions make the psalm louder— more fortissimo. It's a matter of tone. Here are the two brief introductory passages to the Challoner revision of 1750, along with its translation of the first four lines of the psalm:

David's zeal to serve God in the Temple. He encourageth his soul to trust in God.
Unto the end, understanding for the sons of Core. As the hart panteth after the **fountains** of water; so my soul panteth after thee, O God.
My soul hath thirsted after the **strong** living God; when shall I come and appear before the face of God?
My tears have been my bread day and night, whilst it is said to me daily: Where is thy God?
These things I remembered, and poured out my soul in me: for I shall go over into the place of the **wonderful** tabernacle, even to the house of God: With the voice of joy and praise; **the noise of one feasting.**

The King James Bible cranks up the psalm in a different way. The third verse reads: "My tears have been my **meat** day and night, while they continually say unto me, Where is thy God?" In the Hebrew, it is not "my meat," which would be *b'sari*, but "my bread," or *lachmi*. The psalm is about basic sustenance—the survival of the soul; bread is the cheap food of the poor and the desperate. Some translations, like the Soncino edition translated by Rev. Dr. A. Cohen in 1945, choose "food" instead of "bread." But "meat" seems like an editorialization, as if the tears are feeding the Psalmist's faith in a way meant to strengthen it. Instead, the Psalmist has no choice but to eat his own tears as food—that is how far he has fallen.

The question of whether "bread" in fact means "bread" shows up in the eleventh-century Hebrew *Sefer HaShorashim*, or *Book of Roots*, by the grammarian and lexicographer Ibn Janach. Ibn Janach says "bread" means "sustenance," usually the sustenance derived from wheat. Perhaps Ibn Janach's broad definition— "sustenance"—helps explain what happens to the word "bread" in translations of Psalm 42. Yet the use of "bread" in this psalm has resonances that don't work with the generalization. In Jewish tradition, bread is often invoked as a symbol of what God promises man; the *birkat hamazon*, or grace said after a meal, ends with the famous line "I have been young, I have been old, and never have seen a righteous man begging for bread." The word "bread" is associated with what a just man can expect from a just God. I will never forget sitting at a Shabbat lunch in Jerusalem at which several Holocaust survivors refused to recite this line. They had seen just men, hands out for bread, utterly desperate. I think of the kind of desperation those survivors must have experienced, what scenes they must have witnessed, the longing they must have felt

and known, as well as perhaps anger, but also longing for God—
not only to be seen but to act—whenever I reread Psalm 42.

Though Psalm 42 is about longing for God, for me it also
resonates with desperation, and with desire for what is essential
in life even if that essential thing cannot be seen. In that way, it
reminds me, always, of the moment when I was about to travel for
the first time from small town to big city. The psalm is about craving what one most wants—and when I was thirteen, what I most
wanted was to see the bigger world, which was separated from
me by a body of water. The psalm is about wanting something far
larger than oneself, which is what the island of Manhattan felt like
to me then; the city included the possibility of magnificent art and
immense dreams. The Psalmist, too, uses water to express longing, though he describes a deer who wants to taste it, not cross
it. Though the Psalmist does not want to get to know a city—he
wants to know God—for me the psalm is also about whether what
we most wish for is even possible. Of course, of all our wishes,
the desire to know God—to confirm God's existence, and then to
understand who God is and how and why God acts—is probably
the largest and perhaps the most impossible desire. It is far larger
than any city, or any invention of man.

I am no longer as awed by Manhattan as I used to be. I love
the city, but I am now fully able to enter it and leave it, to view
its treasures and walk its streets; I do not continually feel that a
large body of glittering water stands between who I am and who I
want to be on a daily basis, the way I did at thirteen. But on some
days, and at some times, that is exactly how I feel—and I suspect
that is how most of us feel. And that great distance between what
I crave and what I can have returns to me every time I read this
psalm. I again understand that image of a deer craving the edge of

water, the first hint of it. Not knowing whether what is hoped for will happen. It is an eternal sentiment, a deeply human sentiment, because being human is about having limits, about not being able to reach all we want to reach. Being human is about craving. It is, at its essence, a state of thirst.

I HAVE KNOWN BOTH BELIEF and unbelief. I have experienced both sides of the dialogue, the faith and the questioning. I still remember that boy, how his voice rose. I remember how the psalm felt distant and close at the same time as he sang for both the boys and the girls, trying to represent all of us. His melody, and that young voice that knew nothing of what lay ahead, returns to me as I drive across the frozen plains of the Midwest, as I travel around the world with the little book of psalms my grandfather gave me. As time passes, I imagine another boy, my grandfather as a young man. The lone survivor of all his brothers, my grandfather lived a life that mirrored the history of the twentieth century. I know he asked these same questions in his life—*Where are you, God?* or *When will I see God?*—as Europe burned, and his brothers with it, their bodies shot and tossed into a large ditch of a grave they dug with their own hands. Surely my grandfather's soul was downcast, surely he wondered where God was and what God was doing then. For years he left faith, had no use for it. And yet, though as far as I know he never received a direct answer from God, he found a way to return. The psalm, after all its tantalizing twists inside the soul and outside of it, seems to predict this oscillating. It provides a space where we can question, even though it—tellingly—provides no answers. The speaker in the psalm, who was once so faithful and so joyful, as I imagine my grandfather was as a child, gets no answer, but he returns to faith anyway. As for us readers, even if we hear no answer to our own questions, this psalm, incredibly enough, asks us to sing.

I can still remember my grandfather singing loudly in his library. I can hear him praying early in the morning in his kitchen. How and why my grandfather sang in his library and in his kitchen is what is going on in the middle of this psalm, in its recounting of the dialogue deep inside the self, a particular kind of cleansing that is the child of question and song. What is worth singing about is deciding to live in a certain way despite all evidence to the contrary, despite all the knowledge that comes with time: this is what it is to be human, to hope, to believe, to be a repeater of psalms and a singer of them. And like my grandfather before me, whenever I remember these things, I sing, too, loud enough that my soul can hear it.

MEMORY

בָּאִים וְנִשְׂאוּ כָל־אֲשֶׁר בְּבֵיתְךָ וַאֲשֶׁר
אָצְרוּ אֲבֹתֶיךָ עַד־הַיּוֹם הַזֶּה בָּבֶל לֹא־
יִוָּתֵר דָּבָר אָמַר יְהוָה: ז וּמִבָּנֶיךָ אֲשֶׁר
יֵצְאוּ מִמְּךָ אֲשֶׁר תּוֹלִיד יִקָּחוּ וְהָיוּ
סָרִיסִים בְּהֵיכַל מֶלֶךְ בָּבֶל: ח וַיֹּאמֶר
חִזְקִיָּהוּ אֶל־יְשַׁעְיָהוּ טוֹב דְּבַר־יְהוָה
אֲשֶׁר דִּבַּרְתָּ וַיֹּאמֶר כִּי יִהְיֶה שָׁלוֹם
וֶאֱמֶת בְּיָמָי: מ א נַחֲמוּ נַחֲמוּ עַמִּי יֹאמַר

תרגום (right column):
כְּבֵיתָךְ וְדִי גְנִיז אֲבָהָתָךְ
עַד יוֹמָא הָדֵין וְיִתּוֹבַל
לְבָבֶל לָא יִשְׁתְּאַר מִדַּעַם
אֲמַר יְיָ: ז וּמִבְּנָךְ
דִיַפְּקוּן מִנָּךְ דְּתוֹלִיד
יַדְבְּלוּן וִיהוֹן רַבְרְבִין
בְּהֵיכְלָא מַלְכָּא דְבָבֶל:
ח וַאֲמַר חִזְקִיָּה לִישַׁעְיָה
תָּקֵן פִּתְגָמָא דַיְיָ
דְמַלֵּלְתָּא וַאֲמַר אֲרֵי
יְהֵי שְׁלָם וּקְשׁוֹט בְּיוֹמָי:
א נְבִיַּיָא אִתְנַבִּיאוּ
תַּנְחוּמִין עַל עַמִּי אֲמַר
אֱלָהֲכוֹן:

ת"א יותר דבר . נחמו . בקריה ספרים .

רש"י

(ו) לא יותר דבר . מדל כנגד מדה־כנגד לא היה דבר :
ומבניך . הם הנגייה־מישאל ועזריה : (ח) טוב דבר ה' .
מאחר שעימי יהיה שלום

מ (א) נחמו נחמו . חוזר על נביאותיו העתידות לפי
שמכאן ועד סוף הספר דברי נחמות הספסיק פרשה
זו כינם לבין הפורענות . נחמו אתם . נביאי נחמו את עמי :

אבן עזרא

מ (א) נחמו נחמו עמי . לדבקה זאת הפרשה . בעבור
שהזכיר למעלה על כל "קולרות "המלך גם בניו יגלו
לבבל על כן אחרי־זאת הנחמות ואלה הנחמות הראשונות
מנחמי הספר על דעת רבי משה הכהן נ"ע אשר אמר כי

רד"ק

(ו) נחמו נחמו . כל אלה הנחמות עתידה לימות המשיח
והנפל־לחזק ח"י נביאיו אתנבגיאו תנחומין על עמי אמר
אלהכון נחמו נחמו וכן דברו כבו שפירשנום בפסוק חזק ידים

מצאי הספר על דעת רבי משה הכהן נ"ע אשר יש בתוך הספר דברי גלות בבל
לזכר כי כורש שלח העולה ואלה באחרית הספר דברי דברים כאשר אפרש . ולפי דעתי הכל על נלוחינו רק יש בתוך הספר דברי גלות בבל
כי ספר שמואל כתבו שמואל והוא אמת עד יומת שמואל והנה דברי הימים יוכיח ספר דוד וכרוזב והעד
מלכים ירמו וקמו סריס וישתחוו וים להעיר כאשר שמעו וים אינם והמשכיל יבין . ומלא נחמו דברי הנם

מצודת ציון

(ו) סריסים . שרים וממונים :

מצודת דוד

(ו) לא יותר דבר . מכל אשר כביתך : (ז) ומבניך . הם דניאל מנניה מישאל
ועזריה : אשר יצאו וגו' . כפל הדבר בשמות ובלשו כדרך המקראות :
מ (א) נחמו נחמו . אלהיכם יאמר אל הנביאים נחמו את עמי וכפל הדבר על החוזק :

באור — חזון ישעיהו — מלכי"ם **הענין**

(right) בפעם, עד שאחרית דבר יהי' כי הכל ינשא לבבל
אוצרותיך וגם בניך: (ח) ויאמר, אז הכיר חזקיהו כי
השכיל עשר, והודה כי דבר ה' טוב מאד, אם מצד
החכמה שיסתבב מסובבים כאלה מן הסבות בהכרח,
והוא לא השכיל ע"ז מסכלותו. אם מצד הצדק
והעונש על גאותו, ויאמר, כ"ז אמר הלא דבר ה'
על הטובה לא תשוב ריקם בשום אופן. ובזה יש

(left) הבדל בין הדבר שינבא הנביא לרעה, שיכול
להשתנות על ידי שישינו העם את מעשיהם מרעה
לטוב, לא כן אשר ידבר הנביא כש"ה' לטובה שזה
לא ישתנה בשום אופן כמ"ש ירמיהו בן
עזור. וע"פ"ז הנבואה שנבא לו ישעיה פה שיגיע רעה
על בניו, כלולים בתוכו שתי נבואות. א] לרעה על
בניו וזה יצוייר שישתנה אם ייטיבו מעשיהם, וע"ז"א

הערות

[ו] מה היה חטאו שבעבורו נבא עליו העונש הגדול הזה, וכי לא הורשה למלך להראות את בתי אוצרותיו. וכי לא
התפאר שלמה בעשרו לפני רבים עמים. בד"ה נזכר שחזקיה גבה לבו ויהי קצף על יהודה וירושלים. מה
היה זה גבהות לב, והוא עשה זאת לתומו? מה חטאו בניו? מה חטאו אכלו כוסר רשעי בנים תקהינה? האם לא חטאו ירושלים חטאים
גדולים ונאצות גדולות אשר בעבורם הלכו שבי לפני צר, לא בעבור חזקיהו הצדיק אשר הראה אוצרותיו?

[ח] איך אמר טוב דבר ה' יען יהיה שלום בימיו, וכי לא ידאג האב על הקורות אשר יקראו ליוצאי חלציו, ואף כי
אם הוא היה הסבה לקורות האלה?.

נַחֲמוּ
Nachamu
Comfort
[imperative verb]

נַחֲמוּ
nachamu
comfort

עַמִּי
ami
my people/nation

יֹאמַר
yomar
says [literally "will say"]

אֱלֹהֵיכֶם
eloheichem
your [plural] God

דַּבְּרוּ
dabru
Speak [plural
imperative verb]

עַל-
al
on/to

לֵב
lev
heart [of]

יְרוּשָׁלַיִם
yerushalayim
Jerusalem

וְקִרְאוּ
v'kir'oo
and call [plural imperative verb]

אֵלֶיהָ
eleha
to her

כִּי
ki
since [indicates
emphasis]

מָלְאָה
mal'ah
was filled

צְבָאָהּ
tz'vah'ah
her/its task/service/
term of service

כִּי
ki
since [indicates
emphasis]

נִרְצָה
nirtzah
completed

עֲוֹנָהּ
avonah
her transgression/
sin

כִּי	לָקְחָה	מִיַּד	יְהוָה
ki	***lakcha***	***mi'yad***	***adonai***
since [indicates emphasis]	she took	from the hand of/from	God

כִּפְלַיִם	בְּכָל־	חַטֹּאתֶיהָ
kiflaim	***b'chol***	***chatotehah***
double	in/for all	her sins ["Jerusalem" is a feminine noun]

1 Comfort ye, comfort ye my people, sayth your God.

2 Speake ye comfortably to Ierusalem, and cry vnto her, that her warrefare is accomplished, that her iniquitie is pardoned: for shee hath receiued of the Lords hand double for all her sinnes.

Isaiah 40:1–2, King James Bible (1611)

1 Comfort ye, comfort ye My people, saith your God.

2 Bid Jerusalem take heart, and proclaim unto her, that her time of service is accomplished, that her guilt is paid off; that she hath received of the LORD'S hand double for all her sins.

Jewish Publication Society Bible (1917)

1 Comfort, comfort my people,
says your God.

2 Speak tenderly to Jerusalem,
and proclaim to her
that her hard service has been completed,
that her sin has been paid for,
that she has received from the LORD's hand
double for all her sins.

New International Version (U.K.) (Biblica, 1979)

1 "Comfort, O comfort My people," says your God.
2 "Speak kindly to Jerusalem;
And call out to her, that her warfare has ended,
That her iniquity has been removed,
That she has received of the LORD's hand
Double for all her sins."
New American Standard Bible (Lockman Foundation, 1960)

1 Your God says,
"Comfort, comfort my people.
2 Speak kindly to the people of Jerusalem
and tell them
that their time of service is finished,
that they have paid for their sins,
that the Lord has punished Jerusalem
twice for every sin they did."
New Century Version Bible (Thomas Nelson, 2005)

Comfort, oh comfort My people,
Says your God.
Speak tenderly to Jerusalem,
And declare to her
That her term of service is over,
That her iniquity is expiated;
For she has received at the hand of the LORD
Double for all her sins.
Jewish Publication Society Bible
(translation by H. L. Ginsberg, 1972)

Here, deep in the thickness of northern Germany, dogs travel glamorously, in their own spacious compartments. Apart from the dogs, who are large and meticulously groomed, there are only a few passengers on the local train heading north from Hamburg. I see a man with black hair, carrying a leather folder bulging with carbon paper—a traveling salesman, perhaps. There are two old ladies in pastel cardigans, their cheeks wrinkled and stern, and three tanned backpackers, loudly sharing muesli and what looks like bottled carrot juice. Other than that, there is just my blue-eyed mother, nervously staring out the sealed window.

Finally the train swerves out of the station. As the din of Hamburg quickly fades into smooth silence, all we can see is soft green vastness. We are leaving the city, the hustle, the dirt. We are heading to a place two hours past the orange neon lights, fresh fish stands, Turkish immigrant fruit sellers, and prostitutes of the Hamburg train station, past the place where terrorists are rumored to trade visas. We are traveling to see a section of a small city of wheeler-dealer merchants and crusty sailors and their descendants, a place where there were ninety-nine Jews before the war, according to Nazi records, and zero afterward.

I think of this week's Torah portion: *va'etchanan*. The word means "and I have begged God." It is the portion featuring the heartbreaking scene of Moses begging God to enter the land of Israel. I am not sure what I am begging for, not sure what I am even looking for, what land I am about to see.

I do know a few things about Bremen. I know about the Roland statue, the huge medieval sculpture that my grandfather loved as a boy. I know that near the statue there was a fountain, where my great-grandmother would rest with her packages of vegetables before Shabbat. I know, too, that near the statue and the fountain there was a street of artists, where my grandfather, a small Chassidic boy, would go watch the painters. He wanted to take drawing lessons, but that wasn't part of a Chassidic upbringing. Instead, his mother—*meine mameh*, he called her—indulged him by letting him go watch the painters. Just watch.

For as long as I can remember, he has loved color and line, painting and sketching. Since no one else in my family does, I think this love of his went directly into me. I, too, am obsessed with color, moved and motivated by it. I sometimes cry in front of beautiful paintings, and like him, I need to look at them every so often to feel alive, connected to those who came before me.

The most important thing I know of my long-dead great-grandmother is this: faced with the usual wall between Judaism and visual art, she chose to look the other way. She may not have approved of my grandfather's interest, but she allowed it. She didn't say no to a love of painting that competed with the divine. *Atah hachilota l'harot l'avdechah.* It's the next verse. "You have started to show your servant," Moses says. You have started; that is what matters. One of my brothers, Amiad, had this text as his bar mitzvah portion. He sang it, recited it line by line at the dining room table for months. *Atah hachilota*—"You have started." And so here I am, starting.

I am traveling deep into Germany because of my Chassidic great-grandmother, Rachel, whom I never met. She is part of the huge hole of the Holocaust, so I know very little about her, except for the name of the city where she last lived.

I do know several things about Bremen: that the teacher beat my grandfather for being tall and speaking perfect German, that one by one his classmates said "Sorry, Zigmund," and then "Heil, Hitler." One by one they joined Hitler Youth, put on the uniforms and the hats and the boots, and soon my great-grandmother was being beaten right outside her apartment, her groceries strewn on the hall floor. Money was scarce, and the food was crushed. My grandfather's classmates were the ones who beat her, who stomped on her vegetables.

Looking out the train window, my mother and I see graffiti that say NAZIS RAUS: "Nazis get out."

My mother is thrilled. "See," she says, "no one agrees with that anymore."

I am terrified. "If someone needs to write 'Nazis get out,' that means they're still around," I say.

On the local train, I feel stared at, observed. I'm wearing a fuchsia shirt, as usual for that summer, and I suddenly hate my clothing. The old ladies in cardigans look at me intently, and the salesman stares openly. The train clatters, and then, when we least expect it, we are in Bremen.

My mother and I are both silenced by what we see when we get out of the train. We are standing in the Hauptbahnhof, the central train station, the place my grandfather had described hundreds of times as the place he last saw his parents and his four brothers—Yitzchak, Pinchas, Mordechai, and David. We understand what is happening: we are walking into the story.

My grandfather was twenty-two. His youngest brother was thirteen. I am twenty-three. My mother stands beside me. Like my grandfather, I am the oldest of five. I remember the way my grandfather said: "I was just a boy. I was so sure I would see them again. I don't even think I turned around to wave, to say goodbye."

* * *

THE HAUPTBAHNHOF IS CLEARLY THE same as it was in 1936. It
looks as if it hasn't been remodeled for a hundred years. Outside,
it has an ornate curved brick façade, and several carvings of what
seem to be angels. It's hard to see in the sun, but it is certainly
beautiful, as my grandfather described it. Inside, it is huge and
gray and imposing, and the letters on the signs saying FRANKFURT
and BERLIN are old and scratched. I realize that I am standing on
the very platform where my great-grandmother last saw her oldest son. More than sixty years ago, my grandfather left this place,
never to return. And now I, a granddaughter, am coming back,
standing on the same ground.

My grandfather told me how dangerous it was in 1936, when
he left, for an entire Chassidic family to accompany him to the
train station. The trip back must have been frightening, and they
were probably beaten. My grandfather was on his way to Frankfurt, and then eventually to Palestine, on what turned out to be
possibly the last legal boat out of Germany and to Palestine. He
thought of it as an adventure, a year abroad and a way to get away
from the economic troubles of his home city. Like all Jewish residents, by that point, he was not allowed to work. He was not allowed to go to school. The idea of Palestine started because he
had begged to go to school—the unemployed Jewish professors,
including Martin Buber and other luminaries, had set up a university in Frankfurt. My grandfather was starved for education, and
he wasn't alone. Among the young men of Frankfurt, Zionist op-
eratives searched for recruits. "Get out! Get out!" they screamed.
They offered tickets, a new life, a hope of work, and eventually
my grandfather was persuaded.

My mother and I look up at the high, curved ceiling of the Hauptbahnhof. People rush by us; families reunite. Slowly, my mother opens her pocketbook and takes out a carefully folded piece of paper. I recognize the handwriting immediately—the careful, artistic script with the *aleph* that looks like the letter *k*. My grandfather's writing.

"He mailed me directions to the house," my mother says. "He says it's a very long walk from the train station, and we should see if we can get a train to the house."

We walk to the tourist office right outside and ask for a map. When we mention the street name, the lady insists it doesn't exist. My mother looks at the street name, repeats it. Still nothing. I scour the map and find it. Meanwhile, the lady tells my mother that she has a perfect Bremen accent—a comment we will hear again and again, whenever we ask for directions.

It is a huge street, Vahrerstrasse. I can see on the map that it's a sort of avenue. "Oh, that's a long way off—almost out of the city," the woman says.

While I try to figure out where to go, I leave my bag at a counter. Two minutes later, an older man comes out and offers it to me, telling me I forgot it. He is so courteous, so *polite*. I find myself wondering just how old he is. Did he work there sixty years ago, too? Would he have given a Jewish woman her pocketbook back in those days?

My mother and I begin to talk in Hebrew, as we often do, especially when we travel. Suddenly a dark young man comes up behind us and answers us in Hebrew. We are shocked—here, in the most non-Jewish of places, a Hebrew speaker! It turns out that he is a young Israeli who lived in Bremen until he was fourteen, with his father, an international businessman. He asks us what we are doing there, and he is so moved by our project that he offers to be our guide. "I speak German," he says, "and I know nothing about the Jews who were here. I want to come with you."

With him as our guide, we have an easy time finding the trolley stop. It turns out we'll need two trolleys and a bus to get to Vahrerstrasse. So far everything is as my grandfather said. His home *was* very far from the Hauptbahnhof. He said the street was green and full of leafy trees, with a long, narrow center island of bushes. When we arrive, we see several old women—about my grandfather's age—getting off the bus with us. We immediately wonder if they knew him, but we don't ask. They look healthy, aging well and without worries.

It is extremely hot. The street is long, and we're parched. But we continue, amazed that we have come so far. We see the greenery, the thin center island. My grandfather had written: "Look for a house on top of a bar that sells only beer. On the street there will be several bars, and all will sell beer and wine and other things, but one will sell beer only. That is the house."

There are indeed several bars, and we begin to peruse menus. "The Germans live in their houses for hundreds of years, so many of the neighbors should be the same," he wrote. "The landlords are a very mean family. Whatever you do, do not talk with the landlords."

Our guide had no idea that Jews once lived on the street. He tells us that there's increasing commerce here, a strip mall being built. My grandfather said he grew up across from trees. Eventually, we see the outline of a massive Walmart. And then, right across the street, is the house—number 182. On the ground floor is a bar. We walk in to look at the menu, and confirm: only beer.

Suddenly we hear rustling. Above us, a man is in one of the massive trees. His face is shocked, grotesque. "Get off my property!" he screams at us, according to our guide.

"We just want to go to the bar," the guide says.

"It's closed," the man yells, brandishing a saw. "I'll call the police."

He comes down from the tree. Then he sees my mother. His face goes gray, blue, then all of the color leaves. "Who are you?" he says, but it is clear he knows exactly who she is. I start snapping pictures like mad—the bar, the apartment, the yard, the landlord. "I must look like my grandmother," my mother says in Hebrew.

The landlord starts addressing me in German. Because I am tall and have lightened hair, people mistake me for German all the time. I can't answer, so I keep taking pictures. He lunges for the camera, but I'm fast, and I'm young.

"This is Zigmund's daughter," the guide says. "Do you remember the Traum family?"

"No, no, I do not remember them," the landlord says. In his eyes we see that he does.

He looks about seventy-something. "The landlords are mean people, and they had a little boy, with bulging blue eyes," my grandfather had written. I knew I was looking at him.

"I am from Kiev," the landlord says, in his perfect German.

The guide laughs. "From Kiev?"

"Yes, from Russia," he says in an impeccable Bremen accent. "Now get off my property or I will call the police!"

"We would like to go inside, to see where the family is from."

"They are not from here! You cannot go inside!"

I walk to the courtyard anyway. The door to the house is slightly ajar, and I can see a polished wooden staircase. I remember the story that a man from a neighboring town told my grandfather, about how when the Nazis came it was late at night, and my great-grandmother begged to take her *sheitl*, her wig, with her. My grandfather heard the story in 1958 in Israel, after he saw an ad in a newspaper telling anyone from these areas with relatives they hadn't heard from to come to a hotel in Tel Aviv and learn what had happened. My grandfather went to find an empty room and a man from a neighboring village at a table with a white tablecloth. He had climbed out of his own grave, he said, and he saw my family—all four boys, the *mameh* and the *tati*—shot, then fall back into the dirt. My grandfather thanked him and went home, eternally alone.

Suddenly I imagine that they threw my great-grandmother down those very stairs. I click and click; I want to have proof that I have been here, that someone has come back.

After I finish up all my film, we walk to Walmart, buy cans of juice, and then buy more film. I stand in the median of Vahrerstrasse and click until I can't click anymore. The house is quaint—a two-story cream-colored brick house. The upper floor has a porch that is fenced. I'm sure my grandfather will be happy to see the photos.

IN ISRAEL, VISITING MY GRANDFATHER, we wait a whole day to mention the photos. In my grandfather's white concrete house in the Galilee—the house he built with my grandmother with their own hands—we feel we are carrying a pleasant secret, a stash of surprise.

But when we finally pull them out, my grandfather doesn't want to see them. He sits in a white plastic porch chair—moved to the kitchen, right in front of his carefully arranged, beautiful blue drinking glasses—when my mother leans down next to the chair and waves the photos of Bremen.

He waves her out of the way. "Those were difficult times!" he shouts. "Very difficult times! It was a horrible place!"

She takes a step back.

"You do not know!" he thunders.

He thunders for hours. The times and the place, what Germany was. How when he was a boy and Hitler was running for election, his father sent him to hear the candidate, to report back and tell him who Hitler was. How he hid under a bench and heard the future dictator scream a campaign speech. How the crowd was enthralled. Wild, they were, with delight. How he was frightened under the bench, listening to Hitler's campaign and to the crowd's applause.

They *applauded*, he says. They were entranced!

My mother tries again to get him out of the 1930s. "Abba, don't you want to see the statues?"

"Take them away!" he yells.

My fingers riffle through the photos, trying to find the ones where the house looks best.

"I don't want to see it! I don't want to remember it again! You don't know! You don't *know!*"

My mother tries to show him the postcards of tourist sights— the Roland, the fountain, the artist street. It turns out that that street now houses a Paula Modersohn-Becker museum. No, he's not interested. He doesn't want to see any of it. "It was a bad place, those were very hard times," he thunders, over and over again, until I am numb to the loudness.

I decide not to tell him other things. I don't tell him that in Bremen the night we were there, there was a small march of neo-Nazis. I remember one girl in particular. She looked about nineteen, with straight brown hair, fishnet stockings, big eyes with lots of eyeliner. She was carrying a huge sign with a swastika.

Nazi displays are illegal in Germany, but I saw it. I have not forgotten her, the eyes, the stockings, the makeup. I think of her whenever I see fishnet stockings, and I wonder if to be a Nazi is sexy again.

My grandfather asks me to stay a little longer. I stay two weeks, and I hear him cry—*Raachel! Raachel!*—my mother's name, and his mother's name, in the night. His legs, grown purple, show his age, but his large blue eyes are young, his shoulders broad, and the wit still there. We feast, as usual, despite the oxygen tank he now needs. With the thermometer showing 98 degrees, we drink white wine at lunch from his best crystal goblets.

Foolishly, I try to have only one glass. "Eintz is keintz," my grandfather says. One is none. "You must have another glass of wine!" And so I drink. "First-rate," he says. "This winery got first prize with me before everyone else. I bought three cases."

"The wine is delicious," I say.

I know I have to praise the wine; it's part of the routine. The beautiful items must be praised. The beautiful things, these are important.

"Agnon, did I tell you?" he says, referring to the prizewinning Israeli writer. I shake my head, to give him the pleasure of telling me again. "I bought him before anyone else did. He had the Nobel Prize in Literature from me. I was the first."

Books are also part of the *ha'dvarim hayafim*—the beautiful things. It is my grandfather's favorite phrase: *ha'dvarim hayafim*. It takes me years to understand that *dvarim* means not only "things" but also "words," as in *aseret ha'dvarim*, the Ten Commandments.

"Aviyarifka," my grandfather says suddenly. He's the only person in my life who uses my first and middle names all the time, blended together as if they were one. Rivka was my grandmother, his wife, who died of breast cancer at age thirty-six. "We need music, no? I am preparing for the Bayreuth. I know the whole schedule. I have it here, in German, everything that will happen."

The Bayreuth, I know, means Wagner is coming up.

"This is the best stereo, the best. It makes Wagner sound the way he should sound," he says. Wagner comes blaring into the un-air-conditioned heat. My grandfather leans back on the couch in the library, staring at his figurines and singing all his favorite parts aloud. He knows every single word.

Nude figurines stand proudly next to the towering Talmud. Art and religion are friends in his library, and Wagner is welcome to share air space with Tehillim, the Psalms, those poems of begging and comfort. *Ha'dvarim hayafim.* The beautiful things.

I admire his newest acquisition: a wild, super-modern white lamp that literally arcs across the room in front of us. It is impossible to walk across the room without ducking under it. "Just because I'm eighty-four doesn't mean I can't have style," he says. "I saw it, I said, I have to have that lamp. I like what young people like—the newest model, the top of the line. It's beautiful, no?"

"Yes, it's very beautiful," I say, laughing.

"I like beautiful things," he says.

We sit in his library and I glance at his books on Renaissance art.

"Titian is like God," my grandfather says.

"But Rodin—" I say.

"Aaah, Rodin probably studied with God," my grandfather interrupts. "He had to, to learn how to do hands like that. Do you know how hard it is to draw hands? Every bone, every knuckle, every human being different. I have his whole book of hands right here," he says, pointing to the lower left wall. I smile appreciatively at the Rodin book. I remember the artists' street in Bremen and think: This is what he took from Germany—an appreciation of the hand of the artist. Wagner gets louder, and my grandfather sings, sings as if he has never left Germany.

I look just above and count not one but six sets of the complete Talmud. He tells me the library will be my parents' someday, and that each set of the Talmud is for one grandchild. He gives the girls the same books as the boys. None of that religious rhetoric of "no Talmud for women." Just as my great-grandmother Rachel did not close the door for her son, he has not closed the door on art or religious texts for me.

THE NEXT MORNING MY GRANDFATHER is up early, as usual. He's discussing shirts, hats, fabric. Uh-oh. He wants to go shopping. I had almost forgotten in the years since my last visit. No one loves to shop as much as my grandfather. We take a cab to the most elegant store in northern Israel, and he sits in a chair at the front and says he won't leave until I pick out five hundred dollars' worth of clothing. He sits in his stiff elegant hat and his ironed shirt and his long pants, cane on the tile floor, and surveys the bounty. I see him looking at the Italian handbags, the suits, the scarves. He is in a state of pleasure.

I am just out of graduate school, not sure what to do with these elegant items. I can't find much that will work in my life of coffee shops, writing, and teaching, but he insists. We're not going anywhere until I meet my quota. I buy a pair of flowing black pants and a gorgeous brown pocketbook from Italy, along with several tank tops in red and purple. He is thrilled.

"Very beautiful, the beautiful things," he says. "I want you to have some beautiful things from me."

I smile. I know.

"It is important to have beautiful things, and a beautiful environment, and also a beautiful mind. You should have all good things—Torah, and chuppah, and the man who is the answer to the requests of your heart."

I look up and smile. I knew he'd somehow get back to the question of weddings. And I love that he found the phrase from the prayers I love most—*mishalot libech*, the requests of your heart. I think back to my last birthday. The card was, as it always is, a reproduction of a piece of Jewish art. "Aviyarifka, I have been thinking," he wrote in his distinctive handwriting. "All the old people want grandchildren, and then great-grandchildren, and they bother their children for them. I do not want to be like all the old people, badgering you to get married. I have decided this is not right. I will not annoy you about getting married. What I wish for you is *bechir libech*—the choice of your heart."

That night, I model the purchases and he touches the fabric, elated. My brother Davi comes over and we stop talking about silk. Davi knows it's hard for my grandfather to get to synagogue these days, so he sings parts of the Bible for him. My brother does not want to discuss the silk of a skirt, and I will remember that reluctance again in all the years when I am left to think of how different my grandfather was from most men.

Davi chants without a book, the whole thing memorized. We sit outside in the tremendous emptiness of the Galilee, where hundreds of feet separate the white concrete house from the big road. There is no grass in the backyard, no greenery or even the hint of it in the dark of night. There is only baked and charred dirt, the lemon trees and plum trees of my mother's childhood memory.

We listen to Isaiah echo against the dark hills of the night:

Nachamu nachamu ami yomar eloheichem.
Comfort oh comfort my people says your God.

Isaiah 40 moves along the hills like an old man who knows every stone, every weed in his path. My brother's voice is sure, and it is coming out of the air, from his body, from his heart.

Dabru al lev yerushalayim—"Speak to the heart of Jerusalem." *V'kir'oo eleha.* "And call to her." That word, "to call," is the same as "to read." "Read to her," a stranger to Hebrew might think. "The time has come, it is over. She has suffered doubly for all her sins." Then suddenly the lines are talking to each other:

A voice rings out: "Proclaim!"
Another asks, "What shall I proclaim?"
"All flesh is grass,
All its goodness is like flowers of the field."

This section of Isaiah is my brother Amiad's bar mitzvah haftarah. The words belong to us, and they belong to these hills, this air. I sit and listen to Isaiah, a prophet I have loved. I listen to my brother. And then I listen to the darkness, to the hills. "Comfort" repeats; it is an imperative verb. Everything in these sentences is doubled, from the punishment to the soothing, and then the voice itself splits into two—speaker and listener, who are also one and the same. Finally, the comfort of Isaiah 40 is over. My brother and my grandfather fall into conversation, in German, a language that is familiar to me but one I do not speak.

Eventually, we go inside and watch the day's French news,

followed by German talk shows, which are a sleazy parade of mistresses demanding rights and men who admit that they hate children and prefer dogs. My grandfather loves that I can understand the French news, and he happily follows along with the Hebrew subtitles. The last time I was here, I came straight from Paris, after studying abroad as an undergraduate, and he is still in that mindset that I was in then: he loves French magazines, television, radio, and food. I indulge him and watch the French news, which I imagine he has paid extra to receive.

At one A.M. my grandfather is still wide awake, discussing Heine with my brother during the commercial breaks. Both of them sit in their white T-shirts. In the darkness my brother looks like an old film actor, with his thick hair and big, light eyes, with the slow way he moves along the porch, his hand swatting the occasional loud fly.

I have tried to hear Isaiah again as I heard it that night. I have tried to hear it as the only sound for miles, the way it sounds on my grandfather's porch in the hot summer quiet:

Nachamu nachamu ami yomar eloheichem—comfort oh comfort my people says your God.

I have spent five years reading Isaiah intently in Hebrew and in translation, trying to make it mine. And all I have learned from all that labor is that what is interesting to me is the *dvarim hayafim*—the beautiful things, whatever those things are. What is even more interesting is what the English translation of the Bible made me realize: the beautiful things are also the beautiful words. In Hebrew, words and things are synonyms.

The call comes on a Thursday night at the end of October. I'm in my bedroom in Boston, really a living room with huge bay windows that my roommates and I converted into a sleeping space. I am enjoying the thrill of receiving my M.A. in poetry, which was signed and sealed at the end of September—all the beautiful things. When the phone rings, I am thinking that it is beautiful to love poetry, to memorize it. It is beautiful and miraculous that a girl like me can write a poem in English at all. That I have lived, and lived in this way.

"Saba Shmuel died a few hours ago," my father says softly.

And just like that, my grandfather is no longer alive. I write *no longer alive*, not *dead*, not *gone*, because neither of those has really been true.

MY MOTHER CRIES THROUGH THE whole flight to Israel. She doesn't sleep, doesn't eat, sits there fingering her ripped shirt, her sign of mourning. When we finally get to Tel Aviv, my grandfather is not there to meet us. We take a cab he has not ordered, and for the first time in our lives, we have to give the driver—who is not Abed—directions to the house.

I walk in first and cover all the mirrors. Then I let my mother inside, where she sits on the floor. I mourn my grandfather for a week, as is required, and for a year, as is traditional for a parent but not a grandparent. I make a vow, the only serious vow I have ever made and kept, that I will go to synagogue on time every Saturday for an entire year.

I am never anywhere early, barely anywhere on time, but for an entire year I am at synagogue at nine A.M. I want to hear all Five Books of Moses sung aloud, along with every single haftarah, or prophetic portion. I decide that I will say every single word of the Bible out loud, and I will remember my grandfather. I will look again at what he grew up believing, the faith he left after losing his four siblings and two parents to Hitler, and the faith he returned to after losing his wife when she was only thirty-six. I will honor his faith by investigating it; I will respect his endurance; and I will let him teach me something—anything—one last time.

In the snow and the rain, I go. It's a half-hour walk to the synagogue, and I go dressed in my finest clothing—as elegant and glamorous as possible, as he loved. I play with my best rings, thinking how much he had enjoyed the fact that I was alive, that I had lived at all. Once, that last summer, he asked me for a glass of water, even though he was inches from the refrigerator. When I poured him water in one of his gorgeous blue glasses, he said, *"Eizeh ta'anug l'kabel mayim mi'nechda!"*—"What a pleasure to receive water from a granddaughter!"

What he was telling me was: I have a granddaughter; I alone, among my brothers, have lived. I have endured. And I know, as the oldest of five, that the last thing an oldest sibling wants is to be the last one left.

In synagogue, I sit in the back, open a book, and begin my slow task of reacquainting myself with my entire history, with his history, with the beginning. I learn about slave law and animal sacrifices and adultery—artifacts of the past. Slowly, I learn that there are rules and laws, stupidity and wisdom, that there is a space for anger and lyricism and comfort. The Bible covers murder and rape and poverty: it catalogs every kind of ugliness. And it also includes birth and continuity, constant lists of children and grandchildren, those who have survived.

Like many women's sections, the left side of the *mechitza*—the wall, the border between the men's section and the women's section—in the Orthodox synagogue in the Harvard Hillel in Cambridge, Massachusetts, contains many women who sit silently. No one but me reads every word aloud. I am twenty-four years old, and already I am afraid that I will forget my grandfather. I want to possess something he had, to carry it with me.

It gets colder, and I think of the winters of northern Germany, of my great-uncles shivering naked in the snow. I wonder whether they died immediately, when they were shot, or whether they lay there, bleeding, inhaling earth for the last time.

THE CENTURY TURNS. THE YEAR of official mourning is over. I am aware that there was no year of official mourning for my great-grandparents, for my great-uncles.

In 2000, I move to Jerusalem. By the summer of 2001 my brother Davi is living in Berlin, working as a translator. Now he's the age my grandfather was when he left; now he's the curious one. He is the tall strong boy with only life ahead of him.

We talk easily, Berlin to Jerusalem. We are in almost the same time zone. No censors, no threats of death, no returned packages, which my grandfather described as the norm for Germany-Israel communication. Poor, living off grapes he stole, my grandfather scrimped and borrowed to send his starving family in Bremen a salami in 1938, preserved food that could travel. Eight years later, after the war, it was returned to him, moldy, with words scrawled across the brown paper, over my great-grandparents' name and street address: *Address unknown.*

My brother wants to see the house, so I agree to go with him. But my grandfather is gone, and so are the directions. I remember the number 82, and I remember that the house was on a long and green street called Vahrerstrasse and that it was far from the train station, but that's it. Because it's a Friday when we set out for northern Germany, and we cannot travel on the Sabbath, my brother decides we should hurry and take a cab from the Hauptbahnhof. And so for twenty dollars we get a tour of Bremen.

Beyond the castle-like downtown that an Allied bomber did

not want to ruin by bombing, the city reminds me of rows of gin-gerbread houses. The place looks as though it was made lovingly, by a woman with gentle hands. Everything is cute and pastel. It is pretty, well-landscaped, as if awaiting our arrival. There's the gorgeous water, where my grandfather once watched ships sail to faraway lands, and a windmill welcoming tourists to Bremen.

"This is one of the few places where it's bigger now," my brother says in the cab. We both know he's talking about the Jew-ish community. It is one of the oddities of history that there are now a hundred thousand Jews in Germany, most pouring in from the crumbling former Communist bloc. I think of the nineteen-year-old I just interviewed, a Russian Jew who told me his grand-father liberated Germany, and how he thinks of him all the time. He could not have known that his grandson would choose to live among the grandsons of Nazis.

"One hundred thousand people, mostly Russians," Davi says.

Jews in Germany tend to know where other Jewish commu-nities in Germany are. There are no "unknown addresses" in a country that still makes its residents register by religion.

It turns out that Bremen has a new synagogue, within walking distance of my grandfather's old house. Today, the Jewish popula-tion is more than ten times that before the war. Of the ninety-nine, these are the ones who survived: one, my grandfather's cousin, Mary, who survived by walking to Russia, and another, also a cousin, Fanny, by walking to Belgium. Still, as far as the Germans are concerned, everyone is gone. The only survivor to have children who returned was my grandfather. At the new syna-gogue in Bremen, there is a plaque honoring the town's murdered former residents, but none of the new Jews remember them.

How can I complain when I can barely remember myself?

Already I'm wrong about the house. Number 82 doesn't have a bar underneath, and Davi is getting mad. We pace up and down the interminable street, and finally we see an older man, who immediately comes to talk with us. "Can I help you?" he asks, with impeccable courtesy.

My brother begins to ask him—using his perfect German—if he is from the area. "I have lived in this house all my life," the old man says, "and I know everything on this street. But I do not recognize you."

"Oh, I don't come to Bremen often," Davi says. "But I'm looking for an apartment that is on top of a bar that sells only beer."

"Aaah, yes! I know exactly which house you are looking for," the old man says. "It is right across from the Walmart. When you walk, you will see several bars selling wine and spirits and other things. Keep walking, about fifteen minutes, and you will see the one that sells beer only. It has been there ever since I remember. The number is 182."

We know immediately that that's the house. We soon find 182, and my brother sits down on the picnic tables in the front yard. I didn't notice those tables before. I don't see the landlord, and my brother gets comfortable. He's wearing a sweatshirt with Hebrew and English letters on it, from our yeshiva high school in Manhattan, and a baseball cap. It's easy to pick him out as an American Jewish tourist. I'm worried, and a little annoyed that he dresses so dangerously, but my brother doesn't care. Davi takes out a bottle of water and takes a swig.

"This is not a nice place," he says.

It's that swift. He doesn't have to think about it. He doesn't want to see the inside, the staircase, the awful alleyway, the trees.

He doesn't even want to see a German Walmart from the inside. This is not the Galilee, where Isaiah can echo freely off the hills. This is a place that tried to empty us.

We click a few photos, but my brother wants to get out of there. I do, too. We take a bus back to the Hauptbahnhof, which has been remodeled. It's been only two years since I was here with my mother, but the train station is not the same. Between 1998, my first visit, and 2001, my second, a large underground mall has replaced the platform where my grandfather said goodbye to his mother, his father, and his four brothers. The place shines, a gleaming deception.

The past is already buried under a Sbarro restaurant. Even the destruction of European Jewry can be hidden by the same stores that homogenize stories all over the world. The old train station survived the destruction of most of my family, and it outlived my grandfather, but it has not outlived me.

I know now why I came to Germany the first time, and why I returned: I came to look at what I didn't really want to look at. And I struggle to remember it all as it was. I know I must do it, must struggle to remember, even if I don't particularly want to.

I sit in cafés in Iowa City, and then in New York, and try to remember the Hauptbahnhof exactly as it was the first time I saw it, in 1998. And I think of what other writers have tried to tell me about memory. I interviewed a great poet once. He told me of the loss of his father, saying, at first you remember everything: the face and the voice and the man. Then time passes and you forget a little bit of the man. A year and the voice is hazy. And then, suddenly, you forget the face.

I have not forgotten my grandfather's face yet, but I can already feel it happening. It is different with the words of Isaiah: there are official reasons to repeat and repeat them. There is a yearly schedule, a calendar, and in the repetition, there is a balm. *Comfort oh comfort my people says your God.* Young boys are told to memorize what their grandfathers before them memorized, so the words live, even if the boys don't.

Yad hayinu, my grandfather used to say about his four brothers and himself. "We were a hand." And wherever I have traveled, in the years since my grandfather left the world, I have taken two books with me—Isaiah and the Psalms. The tiny book of psalms is always the one he bought, small enough to travel, small enough to fit in my right hand.

HOW IT (NEVER) ENDS

P SALM AFTER PSALM SINGS OF THE MOST ELEMENTAL THREATS —
to the soul and the body. The battles between man and death,
man and God, man and himself, and man against hopelessness
are always present in these most ancient songs. So, too, are a pal-
pable hope in God, a desire for divinity, and a distinct faith in the
continuation of the world. And as I learned sitting in coffee shops
with a stack of Bibles, people not only want to read the Psalms,
recite them, carry them, and give them as gifts to their relatives—
as my grandfather did—they want to talk about them. They want
to make their own personal commentary. And this desire is not
limited to the Psalms; it is true for the Bible in its entirety. The
Bible is the most read and talked-about book in human history;
and since the conversation moved across languages, it is the most
translated as well.

Certainly much is lost in translation, in the attempt to bridge
not only languages but cultures and eras, and while some of these
changes are understandable, others are unbearably painful for a
Hebrew reader to see. The difference in language is not just about
vocabulary and grammar, it is also about culture, about a way of
viewing the world. Yet every translation transmits understanding, and a serious and honest reader of the Bible in translation
will admit to having learned something from biblical translation.
The Jewish sages, in *Ethics of the Fathers*, emphasize this view with
the classic exchange: "Who is wise?" they ask, then answer themselves: "He who learns from every human being." And sometimes, translations of the Bible become essential works in their
own right, great works influencing every corner of literature and

thought in their own language, as the King James Bible has done. There is no perfect translation, because there is no way to bring a text fully from one culture to another, one language to another, one person to another—but every translation attempts to keep a book alive. Generations of translators saw the reading of the Bible as a matter of life itself. Over and over again, Jewish and Christian translators braved everything to keep the book alive, in as much of its complexity as possible. It is important to remember that translators often risked their lives to let the Bible live.

Translations not only impart an understanding of the Bible, they tell us how people of the past read the world in their time: what they thought and what they believed. We should read translations to know how those living next door understand the books we read in the privacy of our own home. And we should also always acknowledge that we are reading a translation—not the original text—and that there is another voice in the room, another mind at work, as we read. What remains from the labors of translators is that the Bible is still with us, still read all over the world.

IT IS NOT DIFFICULT TO imagine the translators' fears for the survival of the Bible, as well as for their own bodies and for the world as they knew it. The Bible itself addresses the question of survival for us, detailing in the story of Noah how one pair of each animal is saved, and how God himself has to open the door to the ark. Dark as the scene of a destroyed world is, the Bible itself is never completely dark; it operates in more than one tone, as life does. And so, while most of humanity is destroyed, Noah survives. And perhaps the story of Noah and the ark makes sense when we think about the Bible's epic journey to us. Noah could not save the entire world; he had to choose, had to bring two of each animal, because only in the plural could they survive for more than a generation. Noah had to leave plenty behind—such as plants, flowers, the grass covering the earth. But Noah makes it, and so does humanity.

Translators throughout time have faced impossible choices. They could not bring everything over in the great journey from Hebrew to another language—and maybe they didn't want to. Perhaps they can bring a lion, but not a flower; an old woman, but not the precise sound of her laughter. And yet, like the biblical Noah, they chose to save what they could, for us.

ACKNOWLEDGMENTS

This book took nearly ten years to write, and in a sense I have been working on it my entire life. It involved the help of many people, in various states and countries, speaking several languages and representing many faiths and points of view. I was taught that *hamevi davar b'shem omro mevi ge'ula la'olam*—attributing what was said to the one who said it brings salvation to the world. And yet there are so many people, such as the librarians in several cities who worked tirelessly to help in the project of reading and rereading, or the many patient coffee-shop workers in several countries who let me sit and write for far too many hours, whose names I do not even know. There are many people, however, whom I could not forget; this is an incomplete list simply because memory itself is imperfect.

Marilynne Robinson was the first reader of what became this book, and the first person in the world to believe it could be a book at all. James Alan McPherson conveyed so much to me about stories, imagination, and humanity. Christopher Merrill and Bonnie Sunstein were extraordinary, helpful, and supportive early readers.

I was lucky to be taught by poets. Deep thanks to Mark

Strand, for sending me on my way; I am unbearably sad that Professor Strand died just days before these acknowledgments were completed. Rosanna Warren's magnificent translation course introduced me to the theory and practice of translation, and her example of excellence and love continues to guide me. Derek Walcott taught me so much about poetry and music that I could not learn from anyone else. Michael Fried taught me to see, and Robert Pinsky helped me understand beginnings and endings.

Cindy Spiegel's brilliance and high standards are matched only by her patience. I could not dream of a more perfect editor for this book. Hana Landes was a wise reader and source of unfailing support; Annie Chagnot graciously helped in so many small and large ways; Greg Mollica and Eric White designed a beautiful cover; and Evan Camfield shepherded this book to the finish line. I am grateful to everyone at Spiegel & Grau for their care and attention to detail.

The fantastic Paul Ingram—a great friend of literature—sent this book on its way; thank you. Paul sent me to Mary Evans, agent extraordinaire. Mary, thank you for believing in this book even when it was difficult, and for being enthusiastic at the right moments.

Thank you to Yiyun Li for all our conversations about reading, for all our bagel lunches and the years of writing they sparked, and to Amy Leach and Matt Lukens for so many beautiful years of friendship.

Several talented friends had an integral role in the development of this book, reading sections and offering to talk about aspects of the ancient, from the tiny to the large. Thank you to Sean Hopkinson, Jeremy Knapp, Mia Nussbaum Alvarado, and Tom Yuill. I am deeply grateful to Ilya Kaminsky, brilliant poet, translator, editor, and reader, for all his insight. Camille Dungy's wisdom and friendship have been a most precious guide for so many years and in so many locales. Special thanks to Brigid Hughes, who read and talked through many incarnations of what became this book.

For years of friendship and love, which could fill a book of its own, thank you to: Curtis Bauer, Sarit Ben Naeh, Sandy Chertok, Scott Dalke, Valerie Duff-Strautmann, Judy Einzig, Rebecca Foust, Laura Gray-Street, Howard Heller, Katrina Kemble, Lili Palacios Baldwin, Rebecca Rosenbaum, Steve Marsden, Tim O'Sullivan, Jebediah Reed, Ira Sadoff, Mariana Vazquez, Aliza Weinrib, Renee Lorence Standing Tree, and Elizabeth Yellen.

The magical Catherine Knepper came into the life of this book at a crucial moment; this book would not be without her grace, wisdom, and talent as reader and editor. I am deeply grateful for the support and friendship of editors: Amotz Asa-El, Jenny Barber, Peter Campion, Sarah Courteau, Jill Jacobs, Miriam Shaviv, Ian Stansel, Peter Stitt, and Nechama Veeder.

The Nonfiction Writing Program at the University of Iowa and an Iowa Arts Fellowship gave me the time and support to work on this book. Special thanks to David Hamilton, Robin Hemley, and Miriam Gilbert, and all my wonderful students at the University of Iowa, who taught me far more than I ever taught them. My gratitude to Connie Brothers at the Iowa Writers' Workshop, a true friend to writers and to literature—and an outpost of the good in the world.

Thank you to the Writing Seminars at the Johns Hopkins University, the Boston University Creative Writing Program in poetry, and the Translation Seminars at Boston University. Thank you to the Ramaz Upper School of New York, and especially to Ms. Rutke Melinek and Ms. Dana Barak, who introduced me to the depth and width of Hebrew literature. My early education at Ashar gave me a grounding in Jewish text for which I am profoundly grateful; a special thank-you to Rabbi Nachum Muschel, my earliest regular reader, as well as my earliest teachers at Bais Yaakov.

A very special thank-you to Bernie Weinflash, z"l, whose wonderful advice and decades of guidance made a huge contribution to my education and the education of my siblings.

Thank you to Columbia College Chicago for its support, and to all my students, from whom I have learned so much. Special thanks to my colleagues David Lazar, Ken Daley, Suzanne Blum Malley, Ames Hawkins, Karen Osborne, Sam Park, and Deborah Holdstein. I am grateful for two Faculty Development Grants for travel to Europe, which helped deepen my understanding of the lives of the biblical commentators.

Special thanks to my Iowa neighbor Pastor Kevin Kummer, and my classmates at the Congregational Church, especially the late Russ Fate for his fascinating questions.

Big thanks to Jerry Sorokin and everyone at Iowa Hillel, as well as Rabbi Jeff Portman, Rabbi Avraham Blesofsky and Rebbetzin Chaya Blesofsky, and Dr. Susan Assouline.

For all-around fabulousness that helped make this book possible, thank you to the Mission Minyan of San Francisco and the Eola Street boys in Berkeley: Barry, Ed, Pablo, Shaun. I wouldn't be walking without Dr. Joseph Stern.

My late editor Doug Delp, for many years of Bankrate.com, made my writing possible, and he helped me think about the intersection of religion and money, and faith and finance. May his memory be blessed. My friend Michael Balch, z"l, loved the prophets as much as I do, and was the source of many memorable conversations when this book began.

The translation community has been extraordinarily helpful,

especially all my friends at the American Literary Translators' Association, the Center for Art in Translation, and the National Yiddish Book Center. For gifts of time and space, and the feeling that writing matters, I am grateful to Ledig House/Writers Omi and the Vermont Studio Center.

And for so many years of all-around marvelousness, thank you to Rachael Wren—I am so lucky to have you in my life, as artist, friend, reader, and cross-country driver.

This book, of course, would never be without my family. I wish my grandfather Shmuel Traum could have been alive to read it, and to place it in his library.

Thank you to Ayala and Kenneth Sachs, for truly being family, and for being my link to my grandparents Shmuel and Rivka.

Thank you to my sister, Merav, for everything, and for being my friend for life.

Throughout the years of writing this book, my brother Davi shared what he knew, and made me question what I thought I knew.

My youngest brother, Daniel, who read this book hundreds of times, is the magnificently talented reader every writer wishes would arrive in her house—which, at many points during the writing of this book, he did. This book would never exist without him.

A special note to my nieces and nephews: I hope you grow to love language as much as your grandparents do; I also hope you will continue the grammar wars, and have them with your children, on and on, forever.

With every year that passes, I feel luckier to have the mother and father that I do. It is impossible to repay parents—only to appreciate them.

Abba and Ima, thank you for your dreams.

APPENDIX A

THE NUMBERING OF THE COMMANDMENTS IN DEUTERONOMY 5

Jewish tradition	Most Protestant Churches, Anglican, and Eastern Orthodox	Most Roman Catholic and Lutheran
1. "I am God" (v. 6)	1. Other gods (vv. 6–7)	1. Other gods (vv. 6–10)
2. Other gods and idols (vv. 7–10)	2. Idols (vv. 8–10)	2. Swearing falsely (v. 11)
3. Swearing falsely (v. 11)	3. Swearing falsely (v. 11)	3. Sabbath (vv. 12–15)
4. Sabbath (vv. 12–15)	4. Sabbath (vv. 12–15)	4. Parents (v. 16)
5. Parents (v. 16)	5. Parents (v. 16)	5. Murder (v. 17)
6. Murder (v. 17)	6. Murder (v. 17)	6. Adultery (v. 17)
7. Adultery (v. 17)	7. Adultery (v. 17)	7. Theft (v. 17)
8. Theft (v. 17)	8. Theft (v. 17)	8. False witness (v. 17)
9. False witness (v. 17)	9. False witness (v. 17)	9. Covetousness
10. Coveting and jealousy (v. 18)	10. Covetousness (v. 18)	10. Covetousness

APPENDIX B

THE BOOKS OF THE BIBLE IN SEVERAL TRADITIONS

The books included in "The Bible"—what Jews call "The Torah" and what Christians call "The Old Testament"—differ from tradition to tradition. The order of the books is somewhat different as well.

Jewish

TORAH: THE FIVE
BOOKS OF MOSES
Genesis
Exodus
Leviticus
Numbers
Deuteronomy

NEVI'IM:
THE PROPHETS
Joshua
Judges
1 Samuel
2 Samuel
1 Kings
2 Kings
Isaiah

Jeremiah
Ezekiel

*The Twelve Minor
Prophets*
Hosea
Joel
Amos
Obadiah
Jonah
Micah
Nahum
Habakkuk
Zephaniah
Haggai
Zechariah
Malachi

KETUVIM: THE
WRITINGS
Psalms
Proverbs
Job
The Song of Songs
Ruth
Lamentations
Ecclesiastes
Esther
Daniel
Ezra
Nehemiah
1 Chronicles
2 Chronicles

Protestant

The King James
Bible — Old
Testament

Genesis

Exodus

Leviticus

Numbers

Deuteronomy

Joshua

Judges

Ruth

1 Samuel

2 Samuel

1 Kings

2 Kings

1 Chronicles

2 Chronicles

Ezra

Nehemiah

Esther

Job

Psalms

Proverbs

Ecclesiastes

Song of Solomon

Isaiah

Jeremiah

Lamentations

Ezekiel

Daniel

Hosea

Joel

Amos

Obadiah

Jonah

Micah

Nahum

Habakkuk

Zephaniah

Haggai

Zechariah

Malachi

Catholic

Canonical Order

Genesis

Exodus

Leviticus

Numbers

Deuteronomy

Joshua

Judges

Ruth

1 Samuel

2 Samuel

1 Kings

2 Kings

1 Chronicles

2 Chronicles

Ezra

Nehemiah

Tobit

Judith

Esther

1 Maccabees

2 Maccabees

Job

Psalms

Proverbs

Ecclesiastes

Song of Songs

Wisdom

Sirach

Isaiah

Jeremiah

Lamentations

Baruch

Ezekiel

Daniel

Hosea

Joel

Amos

Obadiah

Jonah

Micah

Nahum

Habakkuk

Zephaniah

Haggai

Zechariah

Malachi

APPENDIX C

The story of the Bible is a multilingual epic journey. It includes direct translations from the Hebrew as well as translations of translations. These are some important milestones:

Circa third to second century B.C.E.: Septuagint, translation of the Hebrew Bible into Greek.

Circa 110 C.E.: Targum, translation of the Hebrew Bible into Aramaic by Onkelos (35–120 C.E.), a Roman convert to Judaism.

Late second century C.E.: Peshitta, translation of the Hebrew Bible into Syriac; remains the standard version for churches in the Syriac tradition. A signed version from 463–64 C.E. is in the British Library.

382–405 C.E.: Vulgate, translation of the Hebrew Bible into Latin largely by St. Jerome (c. 347–420). This was the first direct translation of the Hebrew Tanakh into Latin, as opposed to a Latin translation from the Greek Septuagint translation. For over one thousand years, this was the definitive version of the Bible for Christians in Western Europe.

Tenth century: Sa'adiah Gaon (892–942), translation of the Hebrew Bible into Arabic. Sa'adiah Gaon was a towering figure in Jewish scholarship and the head of the Sura Academy in Babylon (modern-day Iraq), one of two major rabbinical academies. He was born in Egypt and died in Baghdad.

1382–95: Wycliffe Bible, translation of the Latin Vulgate into English by a group of translators under the direction of John Wycliffe (1320–1384). It was long believed to be exclusively Wycliffe's work, but it is now known that Nicholas of Hereford (died c. 1420) translated a portion, and it is likely that others translated sections as well. More than 250 Wycliffite Bible manuscripts survive.

1530: Tyndale Bible, translation of the Five Books of Moses into English, published in Antwerp by Mertin de Keyser. William Tyndale (1484–1536) worked from the Hebrew and Greek, a first for English translations. Importantly, the Tyndale Bible appeared after the rise of the printing press.

1534: Luther Bible, translation into German by Martin Luther (1483–1546), who worked from the Hebrew and ancient Greek. This was not the first translation into German, but it was very influential.

1560: Geneva Bible, translation into English from the Greek and Hebrew, and heavily reliant on the translations of William Tyndale and Myles Coverdale. More than 80 percent of the Geneva Bible is actually Tyndale's. This was the Bible read by William Shakespeare and John Donne.

1609–10: Douay-Rheims Bible, translation of the Latin Vulgate into English, made in service to the Catholic Church by members of the English College, a Catholic seminary in Douai, France.

1611: King James Bible. The scholars who worked on the King James relied heavily on Tyndale's Bible; some estimates say 76 percent of the Tanakh (Old Testament) and 83 percent of the New Testament is actually Tyndale's.

1749–52: Challoner Revision of the Douay-Rheims by Bishop Richard Challoner (1691–1781).

1764: "Quaker Bible" published in London—the only complete independent Bible translation into English originally published in the eighteenth century. It is the work of a lone translator, Anthony Purver (1702–1777), a Quaker preacher, who worked on it for thirty years. Its official title was *A New and Literal Translation of All the Books of the Old and New Testament; With Notes Critical and Explanatory.* It did not receive official approval from the Society of Friends.

1833: Webster revision of the King James, published by Noah Webster (1758–1843). This revision, sometimes called the "Common Version," modernizes some archaic language and makes grammatical changes.

1845: First Jewish translation of the Hebrew Bible into English, by Isaac Leeser (1806–1868). Born in Westphalia, now Germany, he arrived in America at age seventeen.

1890: Darby Bible. This was an effort to create an English translation for the "unlearned" who are unfamiliar with ancient languages. The Darby Bible was later translated into German, French, Italian, Dutch, and Swedish.

1917: Jewish Publication Society Bible, translation into English. First translation effort by a committee of English-speaking Jews as opposed to an individual translator; chaired first by Marcus Jastrow and then by Solomon Schechter, both of whom died before the committee's work was complete.

1925: Martin Buber (1878–1965) and Franz Rosenzweig (1886–1929), translation of the Hebrew Bible into German. (Gershom Scholem gave a speech in Jerusalem on the occasion of the reprinting of this important translation, saying that this translation was planned as a gift for German Jews, but the "Jews for whom you undertook this translation are no longer alive, and those among their children who escaped this catastrophe no longer read German.")

1926: Yehoash, translation of the Hebrew Bible into Yiddish. Yehoash was the pen name of Solomon Blumgarten, also known as Solomon Bloomgarden (1872–1927). This translation was extremely popular in Yiddish-speaking homes.

1952: Revised Standard Version Bible. This is often used as the official translation in Protestant churches, and was the first major challenger to the popularity of the King James translation. The Catholic edition of the RSV was published in 1966 and it received official approval from U.S. and Canadian bishops as the Catholic translation for private study and devotional reading in 1991.

1966: Jerusalem Bible. The Lectionary used at Mass in England and in most English-speaking churches outside the United States and Canada is based on this translation.

1970: New American Bible. Since 2002, the revised Lectionary, based on the New American Bible, is the only English-language Lectionary that may be used at Mass in the dioceses of the United States, except for the *Lectionary for Masses with Children.*

1977: The New Oxford Annotated Bible with Apocrypha, Revised Standard Version. This is the first English-language Bible to receive both Protestant and Catholic approval. The most recent edition was published in 2010.

1978: New International Version Bible. This is the bestselling Bible in the world, with more than 450 million copies in print. It is primarily used by evangelical Christians. It was most recently revised in 2011.

1985: Jewish Publication Society Bible, translation of the Hebrew Bible into English. "The present version is in the spirit of Sa'adia [Gaon, who translated Tanach into Arabic]," the preface says. Harry M. Orlinsky served as editor in chief for the new translation, with scholars H. L. Ginsberg and Ephraim Speiser as editors, Solomon Grayzel as secretary; three rabbis—representing Orthodox, Conservative, and Reform movements—participated. Novelist Chaim Potok was listed as one of the translators of the Ketuvim, or the Writings.

1985: New Jerusalem Bible. The successor to the Jerusalem Bible, it is the most widely read Catholic Bible outside the United

States. It is translated directly from the Hebrew, Greek, and Aramaic.

1989: The New Revised Standard Version. It is the successor to the popular RSV of 1952.

1997: *The Five Books of Moses* (Schocken Bible, volume I), translation from the Hebrew into English by Everett Fox. Credit given to the approach of Buber and Rosenzweig in their translation into German.

2004: *The Five Books of Moses*, translation from the Hebrew into English by Robert Alter.

WORKS CONSULTED

This is not an academic book but a personal one, and I felt great attachment to many of the writers I read over and over again.

I owe a tremendous debt to the Hebrew commentators on the Bible, in particular Ibn Ezra, Rashi, Radak, the Malbim, the Ramban, also known as Nachmanides, and Sforno, as well as to Onkelos, who wrote in Aramaic. I consulted the writings of the towering Rambam, also known as Maimonides. When a commentator referred to a passage in the Talmud, I went directly to that passage, too. Any errors in understanding their thoughts are my own.

Some of these commentators are available in English translation; others unfortunately are not. As I was writing this book, a new edition of the *mikraot gedolot*, or Great Scriptures, with vocalized versions (with vowels) of all the Hebrew commentaries, was published. I expect this to make life easier for future students of the Hebrew Bible. The edition I used was the *Chumash Mikraot Gedolot HaMenukad*, published by Horev Publishing House (Jerusalem, 2006).

I consulted Nechama Leibowitz's famous writings on the Torah in Hebrew for the Book of Exodus; the title is *New Investigations into the Book of Exodus*, published in 1969. The Hebrew is also available online at http://www.nechama.org.il. An English translation of all of Nechama's work is now available in *Nehama Leibowitz: New Studies in the Weekly Parasha* (seven-volume set), published in 2010 by Lambda Publishers.

The classic multivolume Hebrew dictionary by Even-Shoshan was invaluable, as was the eleventh-century *Book of Roots* by Ibn Janach.

I also learned a great deal from the English translations of the Bible I examined; I list them here.

BIBLES IN TRANSLATION

The Book of Isaiah: A New Translation. Translated by H. L. Ginsberg. Jewish Publication Society. 1972.

The Book of Psalms. The Jewish Publication Society, 1973. (Revised 1997.)

The Book of Psalms: A Translation with Commentary. Translated by Robert Alter. Norton, 2007.

Darby Bible. 1890.

Douay-Rheims Bible. English translation of the Latin Vulgate. 1609–10.

Douay-Rheims Bible, Bishop Challoner revision. 1750.

English Standard Version. Crossway Bibles, 2001.

The Five Books of Moses: Genesis, Exodus, Leviticus, Number, and Deuteronomy. Schocken Bible, volume 1. Translated by Everett Fox. Schocken, 1997.

Genesis: Translation and Commentary. Translated by Robert Alter. 1997.

Geneva Bible. 1599. Reissued by Tolle Lege Press, 2006.

Give Us a King! Samuel, Saul, and David. Translation of Samuel 1 and 2 by Everett Fox. Schocken, 1999.

Good News Bible—Today's English Version. American Bible Society, 2001.

Good News Translation. Today's English Version, second edition. American Bible Society, 1992.

Holman Christian Standard Bible. 1999.

Jewish Publication Society Bible. 1917.

The Jewish Study Bible. Oxford, 2004.

Judaica Press Bible. Translated by Rabbi A. J. Rosenberg. 2005.

King James Bible. 1611.

Names of God Bible. 2011.

New American Standard Bible. 1960.

New Century Version Bible. Thomas Nelson, 2005.

New International Version. 2011.

New International Version, U.K. edition. 1979.

New Revised Standard Version Bible, Catholic Edition. 1989, 1993.

New Oxford Annotated Bible: New Revised Standard Version, with the Apocrypha. Third edition. 2001.

New World Translation of the Holy Scriptures. 1984.

The Psalms. Introduction and commentary by the Rev. Dr. A. Cohen. First volume of the Soncino Books of the Bible. Soncino Press, 1945.

The Psalms. Commentary by Kathleen Norris. Riverhead Books, 1997.

Tanakh: The Holy Scriptures. Jewish Publication Society Bible. 1985.

Young's Literal Translation. Translated by Robert Young. 1898.

BOOKS ON THE BIBLE

Asimov, Isaac. *Asimov's Guide to the Bible: The Old Testament*. Avon Books/Doubleday, 1968.

Lewis, C. S. *Reflections on the Psalms*. Geoffrey Bles, 1958.

BOOKS I FOUND HELPFUL AS I TRIED TO FRAME IDEAS ON TRANSLATION AND WHAT IT MEANS

Daniell, David. *William Tyndale: A Biography*. Yale University Press, 1994.

Grossman, Edith. *Why Translation Matters*. Yale University Press, 2010.

Heschel, Abraham Joshua. *The Sabbath: Its Meaning for Modern Man*. Farrar, Straus and Young, 1951.

Lowell, Robert. *Imitations*. Farrar, Straus and Cudahy, 1961.

Orlinsky, Harry M., ed. *Notes on the New Translation of the Torah*. Jewish Publication Society, 1969.

Schulte, Rainer, and John Biguenet, eds. *Theories of Translation: An Anthology of Essays from Dryden to Derrida*. University of Chicago Press, 1992.

Soloveitchik, Rabbi Joseph B. *Halakhic Man*. Jewish Publication Society, 1984.

————. *The Lonely Man of Faith*. Doubleday, 1965. (Essay first appeared in the summer 1965 issue of *Tradition*.)

INDIVIDUAL ESSAYS ON TRANSLATION I FOUND ESPECIALLY HELPFUL

Benjamin, Walter. "The Task of the Translator" (1923; English translation 1968).

Dryden, John. "On Translation." In *Theories of Translation: An Anthology of Essays from Dryden to Derrida*, edited by Rainer Schutte and John Biguenet (University of Chicago Press, 1992).

Simon-Shoshan, Moshe. "The Tasks of the Translators: The Rabbis, The Septuagint, and the Cultural Politics of Translation." *Prooftexts* 27 (2007): 1–39.

INDEX

ABOUT THE AUTHOR

AVIYA KUSHNER grew up in a Hebrew-speaking home in New York. Her writing has appeared in *The Gettysburg Review, Harvard Review, The International Jerusalem Post*, and *The Wilson Quarterly*. She holds an MFA from the University of Iowa and teaches at Columbia College Chicago.

ABOUT THE TYPE

The text of this book was set in Janson, a typeface designed about 1690 by Nicholas Kis (1650–1702), a Hungarian living in Amsterdam, and for many years mistakenly attributed to the Dutch printer Anton Janson. In 1919, the matrices became the property of the Stempel Foundry in Frankfurt. It is an old-style book face of excellent clarity and sharpness. Janson serifs are concave and splayed; the contrast between thick and thin strokes is marked.